Math Journals

Tools for Authentic Assessment

Vicki Newman

forward by Paul Giganti, Jr.

Acknowledgements

I offer my thanks to the staff, students and parents at McGaugh Elementary School for their support and encouragement. Special thanks to the following for their contributions:

Donna Chafe and Ginger Howard.......Kindergarten Teachers
Sheri Kutz and Virginia Fickes.......First Grade Teachers
Jeanne Schlumpf.......Second Grade Teacher
Jean Huston.......Third Grade Teacher
Jerri Gallup.......Fourth Grade Teacher
Mary Kelsey.......Fifth Grade Teacher
Barbara Wright.......Special Education Teacher
Lois Cohn.......Media Center Teacher
Elizabeth Bardar.......Reading Specialist
John Blaydes.......Principal

Published by
Teaching Resource Center
P.O. Box 1509
San Leandro, CA 94577

Edited by Jan Goodman.
Design and production by Janet Piercy and Janis Poe.

Printed in the United States of America.
ISBN: 1-56785-033-2

Contents

Forward

Writing opens up a window into the mind. For the writer, no other form of communication is as precise and reflective as the written word. Putting ideas in writing requires the author to question, review and refine his or her own thoughts. E.E. Forster once wrote, "I don't know what I think until I see what I've said." For this reason and more, writing is a very special human endeavor.

For teachers, writing can open up windows into their student's minds. Writing can be both a powerful teaching and assessment tool. It allows teachers to "see" a student's thought processes, to "hear" what the student thinks he or she heard, and to "feel" some of the emotions that accompanies an individual's success or failure to understand new concepts and ideas. These dual benefits, for the writer and for the teacher, make writing an extremely powerful device for teaching and learning.

Writing is a relatively new tool in the hands of mathematics teachers at all levels. Writing and mathematics may seem like strange bedfellows, but there are as many valid applications of writing in mathematics as there are in the language arts, literature and social studies curricula. The current changes in mathematics curriculum, instruction and assessment, as advanced by the National Council of Teachers of Mathematics, in its publication, *Curriculum and Evaluations Standards for School Mathematics,* have created a climate and environment in mathematics classrooms, kindergarten through grade 12, for new and much needed forms of authentic assessment of children's knowledge and understanding of mathematical ideas.

Vicki Newman has written a book that will guide teachers in the uncharted waters of writing in mathematics, and assist those teachers already making efforts to write in their math classes with new and creative ideas to enhance any mathematics program. *Math Journals* can serve many purposes. It can help teachers learn to use writing as a process in implementing the new *Standards*-based mathematics curriculum; it can guide teachers already familiar with language curriculum portfolios in making the bridge to mathematics portfolios and journals; and it can demystify and comfort teachers in making the transition to authentic assessment.

The lessons, teaching ideas and assessment techniques introduced in *Math Journals* can be valuable in implementing a writing-in-math program. Vicki's use of children's literature as a springboard to problem-solving activities, her use of open-ended questions that promote student writing, and a clear, easy-to-follow format, make *Math Journals* a useful addition to any teacher's resources. As well, Vicki's frequent use of samples of actual student writing lend the lessons a special air of reality and should give teachers added motivation to do the activities with their own students.

Students will be called upon more and more often in the future to express their thoughts and understanding in writing in all curricula. The time to begin to learn the process of writing in mathematics is not when confronted by the sudden need to explain one's understanding on a test. Teachers will do their students a great service by implementing a writing-in-math program in their classroom. This magical process will benefit both student and teacher alike.

Paul Giganti, Jr.
Director, Bay Area Math Project
Lawrence Hall of Science
University of California, at Berkeley

Introduction

This book will help teachers use journals to integrate authentic assessment with the instruction of mathematics. It provides a structure to encourage students to write regularly in mathematics. The book will help teachers develop their own assessment questions and activities for additional mathematical explorations. For each grade level, the book includes the following activities that culminate in journal writing:

Questions For Reflection: these questions are presented at each grade level at the beginning of the school year. They are used to assess students' prior knowledge, attitude about mathematics, and their ability to describe their thinking. At the end of the school year, similar questions are posed again to assess the students' growth over time. Student responses to reflection questions also help teachers assess the effectiveness of their mathematics program. In Grades K–2, literature is used as a springboard for reflection questions. This activity should take one or two days.

The questions help children focus on their mathematical learning experience. They are aligned with standards from the *National Council of Teachers of Mathematics* (NCTM). In Grades K–2, the questions focus on the area of number because they are an element of every area of mathematics. *Questions for Reflection* will provide insights in the following areas, as specified by NCTM:

- Numbers can be used to solve problems in the real world.
- Numbers are used in all strands of mathematics.
- Numbers are used to count objects. (one-to-one correspondence)
- Numbers can be used to describe quantities of whole objects or parts of a whole.
- Numbers can be changed by combining two groups of objects or splitting up a quantity into parts. (addition or subtraction)
- Numbers do not change if the arrangement varies.
- There is a sequence for the counting numbers. (patterns and relationships)
- Words like *more, less* and *same* help to describe the size of quantities in comparison to other quantities.
- Quantities can be represented through grouping and place value.
- Data can be organized into graphs and tables making mathematical ideas easier to comprehend.

In Grades 3–5, *Questions For Reflection* will provide insights in the following areas, as specified by NCTM:

- *Mathematics as Problem Solving*
  Students' ability to develop and apply strategies to solve a variety of mathematical problems in the real world.
- *Mathematics as Communication*
  Students' ability to clarify thinking about mathematical ideas. Physical materials, pictures and diagrams can be related to mathematical ideas. Organizing data into graphs and tables make mathematical ideas easier to comprehend.
- *Mathematics as Reasoning*
  Students' ability to draw logical conclusions about mathematics, justify their thinking and discuss alternative approaches; to use patterns and relationships to analyze mathematical situations.
- *Mathematical Connections*
  Students' ability to recognize that mathematical concepts can be connected to help them gain mathematical understanding.

Math Explorations: Each chapter contains two explorations where students work individually or collaboratively to solve open-ended problems, guided by discussion questions. Students use journals to present their solutions in words, pictures, diagrams, graphs, or symbols; and to explain their strategies and evaluate their results. Each exploration is introduced by a related literature selection. Extensions for explorations are included at the end of each chapter.

Exploration 1 at each grade level illustrates a "unit" approach to develop a mathematical concept. A series of activities are described that integrate related areas of mathematics. When the activities are complete, students respond to discussion questions in their journals. These activities may take as long as one month.

Exploration 2 at each grade level contains one open-ended question that requires students to apply their mathematical knowledge in problem-solving situations. After the problem is solved, solutions are shared and students respond to discussion questions in their journals. This activity may take two to five days depending on the needs of the students.

Why Change? A Teacher's View

One of the major issues confronting educators today is how to prepare our students for a rapidly changing age of technology. This requires us to evaluate our philosophy and attitudes—to look at the content we are delivering to students and the teaching strategies that we use. We need to make sure that as technology evolves, our curriculum evolves along with it so that our students will truly be prepared for the world that they will face when they leave school.

While evaluating my philosophy and attitudes, one of the areas that I knew I wanted to further explore was that of mathematics. As an elementary classroom teacher who loves math, I believed in the equation: *Mathematics Minus the Mystery = Success For All.*

I also believed that a student who has a good understanding of mathematics will be well prepared to face the challenges of technology and of the future.

For guidance, I turned to sources such as the *Curriculum and Evaluation Standards for School Mathematics* and the *Professional Standards for Teaching Mathematics,* written by the *National Council of Teachers of Mathematics (NCTM).* These standards validated the program that I had been developing around three important objectives for students: (1) to become mathematical problem solvers, (2) to develop a picture of mathematics, and (3) to apply math concepts in real-life situations.

As my students became more involved in a problem solving approach to mathematics that centered around real-live experiences, I saw that they were able to generate more language exchange which in turn led them to a variety of mathematical discoveries. When they made discoveries in this way, they displayed a greater understanding and more ownership in those understandings.

I was pleased and excited about the way my students were interacting with mathematics, but I became concerned about how to assess and evaluate their mathematical thinking. Traditional assessment tools did not provide an authentic assessment of my students' understanding of mathematics nor of their ability to apply that knowledge. After administering a traditional test, I would often need to have conferences with students to find out whether their errors were in computation or conceptual understanding. When I spoke with students individually, I was able to gain more information about their mathematical thinking.

Although I valued these individual student conferences, I realized that I would only be able to meet with students occasionally because of the number of students in my class. That is why I decided to use math journals to have students put their thoughts, discoveries and questions down in writing. When they put their thinking down on paper, I was able to gain the information I was looking for without meeting with each student individually. Those original journals have evolved into this book, *Math Journals: Tools for Authentic Assessment.*

Through the writing, pictures and diagrams that students produce in their journals, they are able to:

- Show how their mathematical thinking is developing
- Use mathematical language to communicate discoveries
- Reveal any misunderstandings and why they occur
- Express their attitude toward mathematics

When I first began using math journals in my classroom, my students were reluctant to write. However, after reassurance that their thinking was valued, they learned to write with confidence and enthusiasm. I consistently asked probing questions to help students focus on mathematical concepts and encouraged them to express their thinking. Since my assessment was now integrated with instruction, I was able to focus more easily on what students understood and could do rather than what they didn't know or couldn't do. Authentic assessment became such an integral part of instruction that traditional assessment methods became unnecessary.

Parents were pleased to have the opportunity to see and discuss their children's math journals during parent/teacher conferences. Parents felt they were able to gain greater insights into their children's understanding of mathematics and to see how they performed in a variety of problem solving situations. The journals also demonstrated how the students adapted to the changes in the mathematics curriculum and helped parents become more comfortable and receptive to new teaching and learning techniques.

The math journals described in this book have become an invaluable assessment instrument in helping everyone involved—student, teacher and parent—better evaluate mathematical understandings and establish future goals.

Writing In Math Journals

When children learn that their thinking is valued they feel more confident with journal writing. This can be a slow process that requires your persistence and patience. For most children, writing in mathematics will be a new experience. At the beginning of one particular school year, I remember a student who appeared to be actively engaged in the writing process. However, when I read his journal entry, I found he had written all the questions and two or three word responses. By the end of the school year, he was writing a full response to each question.

The Pre-Writing Stage

It is important to spend a lot of time during the pre-writing process to develop a child's mathematical language through real-life problem solving experiences.

The Role of a Teacher as Facilitator of Learning

As children use their own language to make discoveries, help them connect their ideas with appropriate mathematical language to strengthen their understanding of mathematical ideas. By the time students are asked to write in their math journals, they should be comfortable with the language used during the math exploration.

The Pre-Writing Stage

During the pre-writing stage, emphasis should be placed on:

- Real-life experiences
- Oral language
- Group work
- Problem solving
- Manipulatives
- Calculators
- Literature

The Teacher's Role

To establish your role as facilitator of learning, encourage children to:

- Ask questions
- Describe observations
- Generate predictions
- Make estimations
- Explain strategies
- Communicate discoveries
- Evaluate results

How to Create a Mathematically-Rich Learning Environment

The classroom should be rich in mathematical print. As students share their ideas, record their thoughts on the board using diagrams, pictures, graphs, charts and symbols. Children need to see that their ideas can be transferred into print. Demonstrate how to make a *word web* or *Venn diagram* to help students cluster their ideas during the pre-writing stage.

Word Web

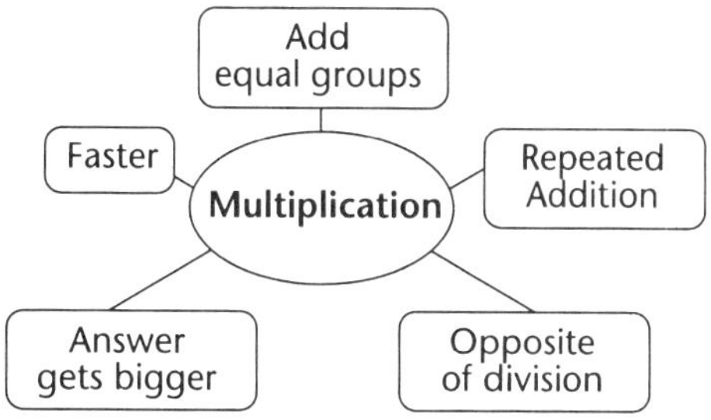

Venn Diagram

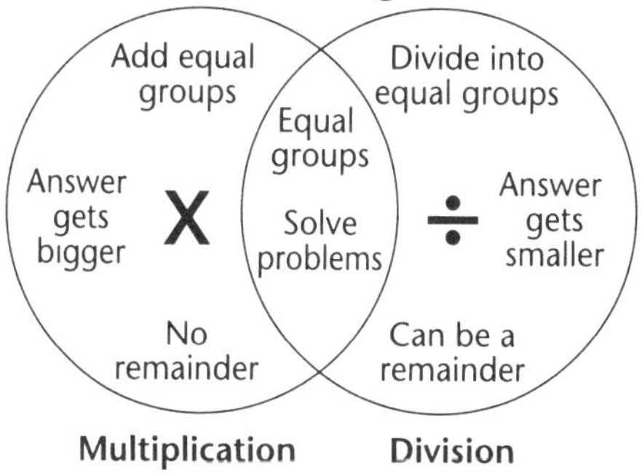

Math Journal Writing

In order for students to become proficient with journal writing, it is important that they write in their math journal at least two to three times a month. Suggestions for other assessment questions are included in this book at each grade level.

After students have completed the activities during the pre-writing stage, write all the assessment questions on the board or chart paper so that students can discuss the questions as a total group before responding in their math journals. Make a word bank with all the mathematical vocabulary that is generated during the discussion so that students can use these words in their journal entries. Encourage students to share their thoughts in complete sentences. Children can underline words that they are not sure how to spell, if they want the word to be corrected. Here are some other suggestions to assist students during their writing experience:

Kindergarten – First Grade	Second – Fifth Grade
Use paper without lines to construct a math journal for each student. (First grade students can use paper with lines.)	Use a spiral notebook or construct a math journal for each student.
Write a class entry to model for students how to answer the questions before they respond in their math journals.	If students have never used a math journal, write a class entry to model for students how to answer the questions before they respond in their math journals.
Each entry should be dated to show growth over time.	Students should date each entry to show growth over time.
Make a copy of each question for students to glue in their journals.	Students can write the questions, glue a copy of the questions in their journals, or just respond to each question.
Provide a given time period (10–20 minutes) for all students to respond to the questions in their journals. Allow more time if needed. ⋆ Questions could be answered during different sessions rather than all at once.	Provide a given time period (15–45 minutes) for all students to respond to the questions in their journals. Allow more time if needed. ⋆ Questions could be answered during different sessions rather than all at once.
Encourage students to use diagrams, pictures, charts, graphs, and symbols to support the writing process. ⋆ Students can dictate sentences to go with their representations.	Encourage students to use diagrams, pictures, charts, graphs and symbols to support the writing process.

Teachers need to respond to each math journal entry. Comments should encourage mathematical language, understanding and thinking to help students view themselves as mathematicians. Allow time for students to edit and make revisions, if necessary. Together, teacher and student can choose journal entries as samples to be placed in an individual portfolio. Original drafts, revisions and final versions could be included, if desired.

How To Assess Mathematics Journals

Discussion questions and questions for reflection must be chosen carefully to elicit journal responses that help you assess students' mathematical understanding. For example, after students have worked in a problem solving situation, applying mathematical concepts to solve an open-ended problem, have them respond to questions that reveal how well they can think, solve and communicate their ideas:

- What was the problem?
- How did you solve the problem?
- What strategies did you use?
- Is there another way you could have solved the problem?
- What mathematics did you learn?
- How did you work cooperatively with other group members?
- How did you feel about the problem? Why?

Before you can assess each student's journal entry, it is important to know what kind of responses you are looking for. You need to think about what elements would make a good answer. If a student is asked to respond to the question, "What is multiplication?", a thorough response should include the idea that multiplication means counting equal groups. It doesn't matter whether the student uses words, pictures, charts, or diagrams in the answer, but this idea must be communicated effectively for a thorough response.

Assessment of journals can be formal or informal.

An informal assessment can be:

- A written response or brief comment from the teacher, which could include praise for the elements of the entry which closely match the standards she has set up, as well as, suggestions for improvement.
- A self-assessment by the student, after the student has compared his or her journal with a partner's or members of a small group, or after a few journals have been shared with the entire class.

More formal means could include:

- Sorting papers into high, medium and low responses
- Attaching a 4 x 6 card, folded in half. List *evidence of strength* on one side and *areas for improvement* on the other side.
- Developing a checklist that lists standards for a high response. Use it to grade particular entries (example below) and give the entry a 3 (total) 2 (partial) or 1 (minimal) for each student.

Checklist	3	2	1
Demonstrates an in-depth understanding of concepts			
Demonstrates an in-depth understanding of content			
All questions are answered completely			
Mathematical ideas are communicated effectively and clearly			

In this book, a short narrative is used to assess each sample journal entry. This is another, more informal way, to evaluate mathematical understanding.

An Overview: Grade Level Lessons

Grade	Questions For Reflection	Math Exploration 1	Math Exploration 2	Questions For Reflection
K	**What I Already Know About Numbers** *One Yellow Lion*	**Shapes: Plane Figures** *A Fishy Shape Story*	**How Many Ways?** *Moon To Sun*	**What I Learned About Numbers** *One Watermelon Seed*
1	**What I Already Know About Numbers** *Ten Black Dots*	**Money** *Dollars and Cents for Hariett*	**How Many Feet?** *How Many Feet in the Bed?*	**What I Learned About Numbers** *Demi's Count the Animals 1-2-3*
2nd	**What I Already Know About Numbers** *10 for Dinner*	**Measurement: Length** *Jim & the Beanstalk*	**More Than, Less Than or Twice As Many?** *The Baby Blue Cat & the Whole Batch of Cookies*	**What I Learned About Numbers** *Two Ways to Count To Ten*
3rd	**What I Already Know About Mathematics**	**Geometric Solids** *If You Look Around You*	**Eight Dinner Elsie** *Six Dinner Sid*	**What I Learned About Mathematics**
4th	**What I Already Know About Mathematics**	**Multiplication** *Sea Squares*	**How Many Rabbits?** *The April Rabbits*	**What I Learned About Numbers**
5th	**What I Already Know About Mathematics**	**Fractions** *Eight Hands Round*	**Baker's Dozen** *The Baker's Dozen*	**What I Learned About Numbers**

Kindergarten

Questions for Reflection

Literature Connection: *One Yellow Lion* by Matthew Van Fleet
This counting book begins with one yellow lion and ends with ten pink worms as you flip open each page. At the end of the book, all the animals appear together.

1. At the beginning of the school year, pose the following questions:

Questions For Reflection
What I Already Know About Numbers • What do you know about numbers? • How do you use numbers each day?

2. Have students discuss the questions as a total group. Record their ideas on the board.
3. Tell students that you are going to read a story about numbers. Ask them to listen carefully to see if there is anything they can add to their list about what they know about numbers.
4. Read orally *One Yellow Lion.*
5. After reading the story, choose some of these questions to discuss:

Questions To Ask	Possible Answers
How were numbers used in the story?	• To show how many gray squirrels there were. • To show that there was one yellow lion. • To count how many animals there were.
How many purple lizards were there?	• Seven
How do you know there were seven purple lizards?	• There is a number "seven." • You can count the lizards.
Were there more red roosters or blue whales?	• There were more blue whales.
How do you know there were more blue whales than red roosters?	• You can count them. • 5 is one more than 4
What can you tell us about the number 3?	• There are three gray whales. • You count 1-2-3 when you count the whales.
How can we find out how many lions and swans all together?	• Count • 1 + 2 = 3
We talked about how the book used numbers. How do you use numbers each day?	• To tell how old I am. • To count the people in my family. • To measure how tall I am.
What do you know about numbers?	• 6 is bigger than 5. There are 5 fingers on my hand.

6. Review the *Questions For Reflection* and add new ideas to the list on the board.
7. Write a class journal entry modeling how to answer the questions. Discuss how this is just one way to answer the questions. Students can share other ways.
8. Have students answer the questions in their journals.
   ★ *Encourage students to use diagrams, graphs, pictures and symbols to help explain their answers. You can have students dictate sentences to with their representations.*
9. The journal entries will give you information about:
   - students' understanding of the numeration system.
   - their number sense.
   - how they use numbers in the real world.
   - their understanding of the concepts of whole number operations.
   - their attitude towards mathematics.
10. Save the journal entries and use them to compare each student's response to questions for reflection at the end of the school year. (See *From the Classroom,* page 25.)
11. **Optional:** Students can make their own class counting books following the pattern in the story. For example, the book could be called *One Orange Pumpkin.*

Math Exploration 1: Plane Figures

Literature Connection: *A Fishy Shape Story* by Joanne and David Wylie
When her friends ask questions about the fish she caught, a child uses words such as *circle, square, rectangle* and *crescent* to describe the shape of each fish.

1. Tell students they will be studying shapes. Show them some shapes and ask these questions:
   - What do you know about these shapes?
   - Where are some other places in the room that you see these shapes?
2. Remind students to listen carefully as you read *A Fishy Shape Story* so that you can talk about how shapes were used in the story.
3. After reading the story, ask these questions:

Questions To Ask	Possible Answers
How were shapes used in the story?	• To make different fish.
What shapes were used in the story?	• Oval • Square • Crescent
Can you think of something in real-life that is shaped like a circle?	• Moon • Pancake
Tell about a square.	• It has sides. • It has corners.

4. During the unit on shapes, provide these hands on opportunities:
   - Students draw their own fish using one of the shapes. Then they can write about their fish. This can be placed in a class big book.
   - Have children help outline different shapes on the carpet with tape or string. Let them walk around each shape to recognize how many sides and corners.
   - Students can match plane figures (2-dimensional) with faces of geometric solids (3-dimensional).
   - Have students design a picture using pattern blocks and identify which shapes were used.
   - Place attribute blocks in a bag. Have a student describe one block in the bag by feeling the shapes without looking. The other students can guess the shape of the block.
   - Students can cut out pictures from a magazine that represent different shapes and make their own shape book.
   - Ask students to describe how shapes are alike and different. (Use pattern blocks, attribute blocks, paper shapes, etc.)
   - Have students find different ways to sort and classify the shapes. (Shapes that have sides and no sides; shapes that have corners and no corners.)
5. After completing the unit on shapes, give each pair of students a copy of the Activity Sheet K-A. The attributes of size and shape are represented on the sheet. Students can color the shapes to add a third attribute. Each pair needs to cut out the shapes, decide how to sort and classify the shapes, and glue them on a piece of construction paper to show how they sorted the shapes.
6. Each pair of students needs to share how they sorted the shapes during a class discussion. Students talk about all the different ways to sort and classify the shapes.

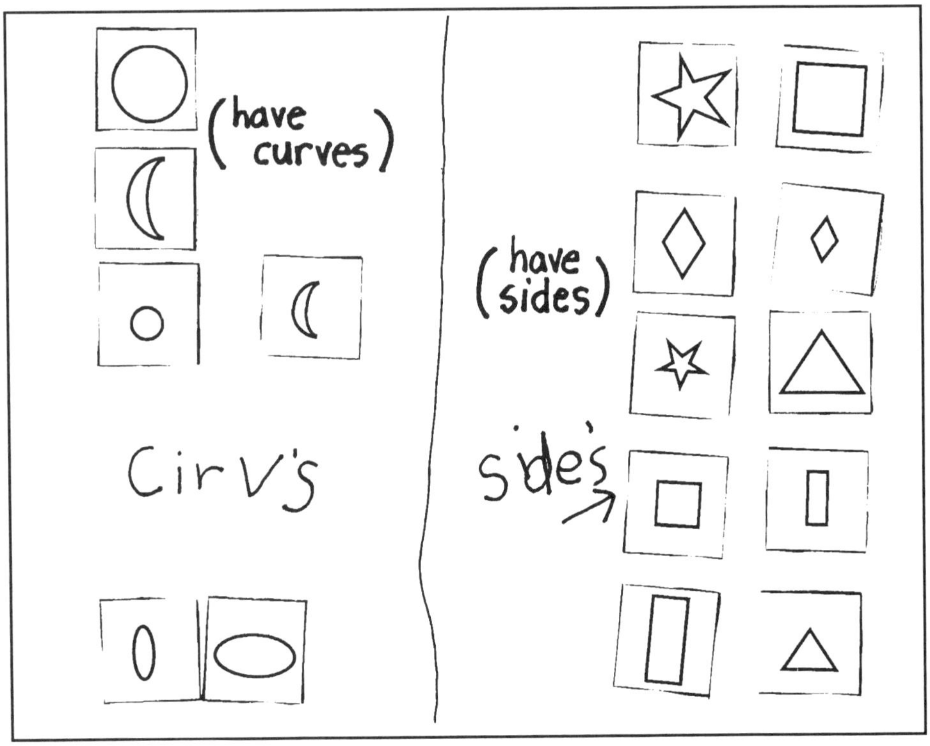

From the Classroom:
Kindergarten

Here, the student sorts the shapes and is able to clarify her mathematical thinking. The task requires the student to reason mathematically and define attributes.

7. When the unit on plane figures is complete, pose the following questions about plane figures:

Discussion Questions: Plane Figures
• What did you learn about shapes? • How are your shapes alike and different? • How did you sort your shapes?

8. Write a class journal entry modeling how to answer the questions. Discuss how this is just one way to answer the questions. Students can share other ways.
9. Have students answer the questions in their journals.
   ★ *Encourage students to use diagrams, graphs, pictures and symbols to help answer the questions. You can have students dictate sentences to go with their representations.*
10. Use journal entries to assess students' level of understanding of plane figures and their ability to express what they know. The examples on the following four pages demonstrate a range of student responses that is likely to occur in your classroom.

From the Classroom: *Sample K–1*

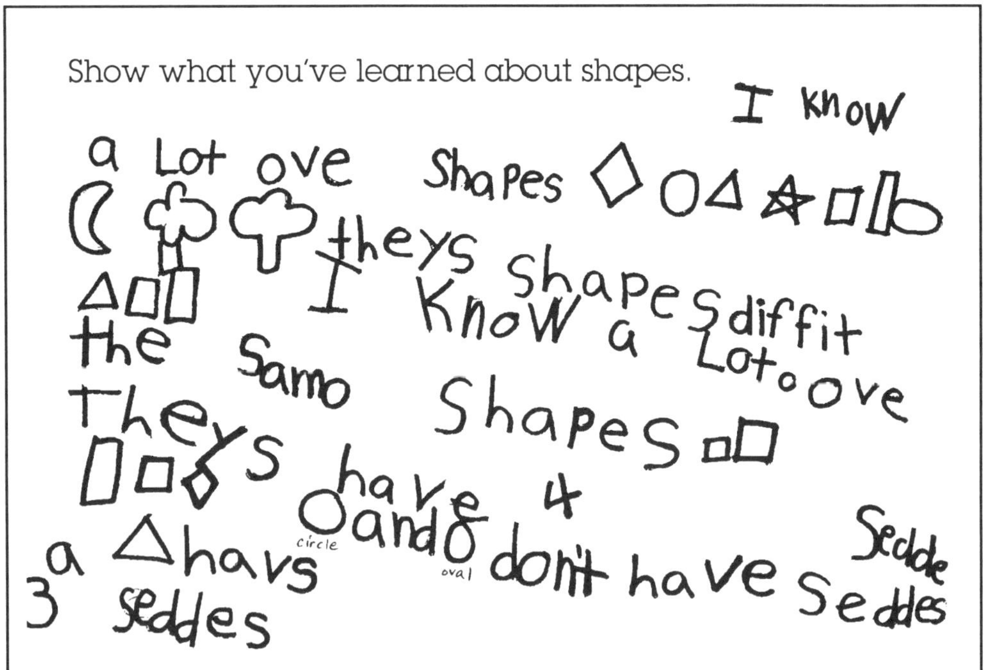

Translation: I know a lot of shapes. These shapes are different (◊❑❍△). I know a lot of the same shapes (▫❑◊). They have 4 sides (❑▫◊). A circle and an oval don't have sides. A triangle has three sides.

page 1

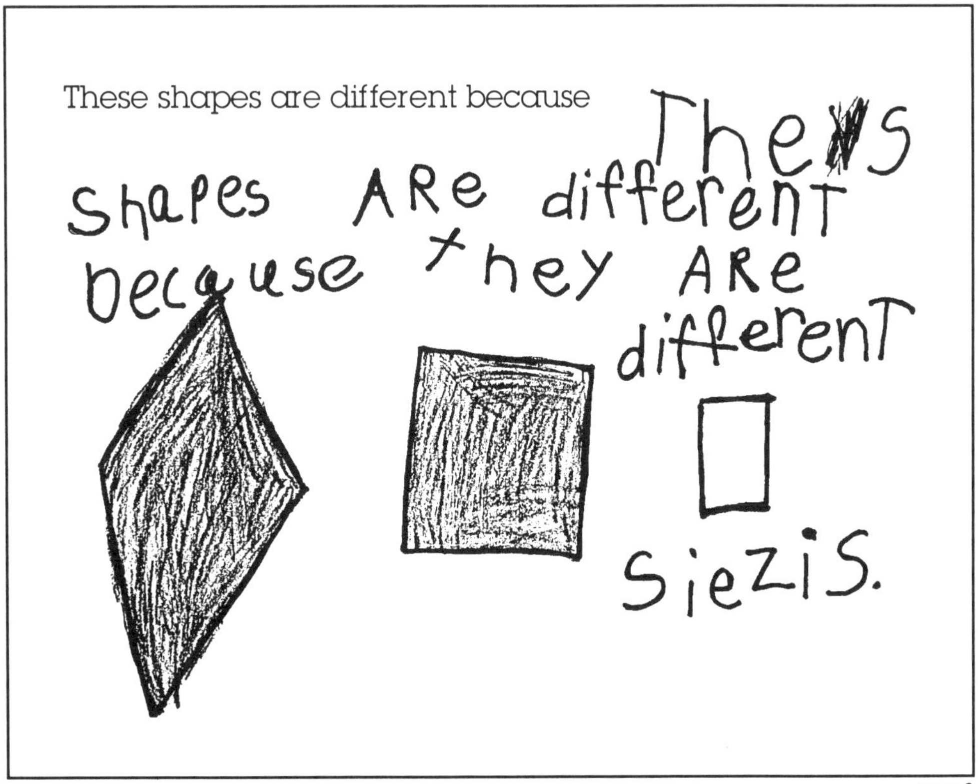

page 2

In this sample, the student shows a thorough understanding of plane figures. She is able to communicate effectively with diagrams, pictures, symbols and some words. All questions were answered and she successfully sorted her shapes and classified them by the number of corners.

These shapes are similar because They have
All CORnz.
they all have corners.

page 3

5 CORnz
4
3 CORnz
0 CORnz
(corners)

page 4

page 1

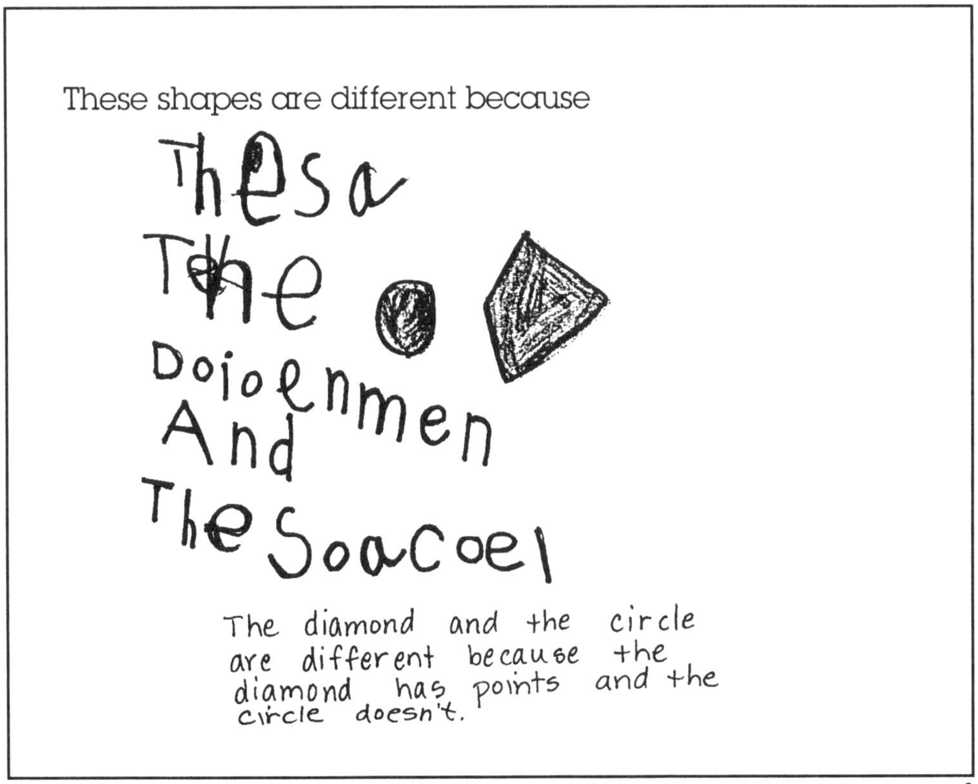

page 2

In this sample, the student demonstrates some knowledge of plane figures but does not always use appropriate math vocabulary. He successfully sorted his shapes and classified them by size. However, the way he sorted his shapes was not as sophisticated as sample K–1.

These shapes are similar because
TheYall
Have colers
they all have colors.

page 3

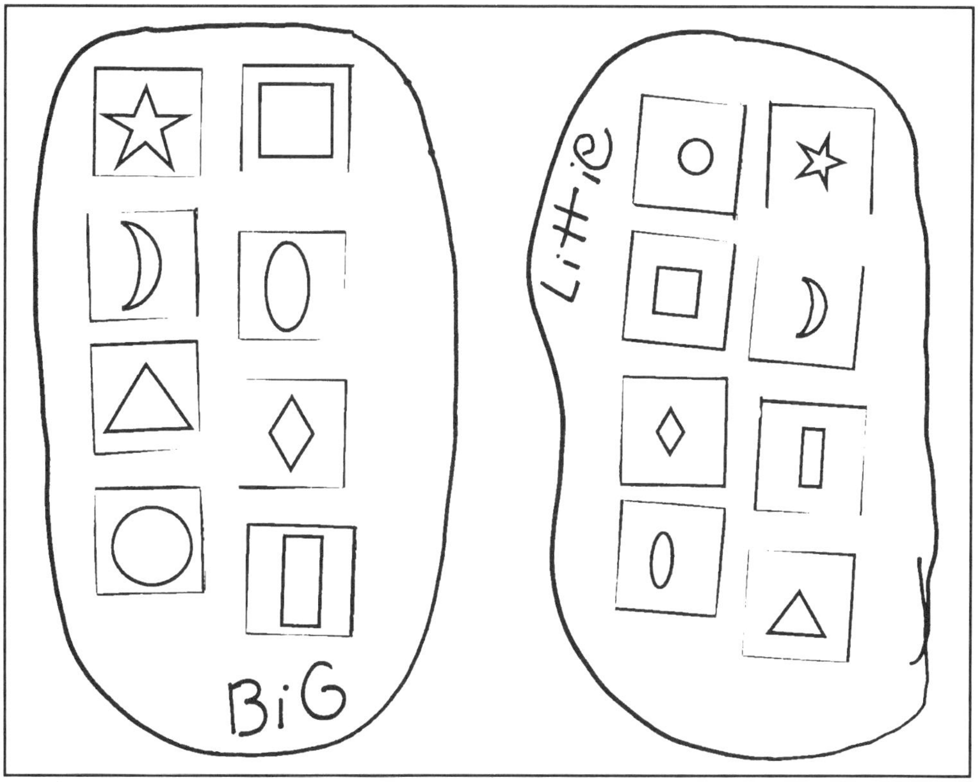
Little
BiG

page 4

Shapes

Cut out the boxes and sort the shapes.

Math Exploration 2: How Many Ways?

Literature Connection: *Moon to Sun* by Sheila White Samton
This addition book begins with one moon and ends with one sun to represent the night as it turns to dawn. Each picture helps the reader add to ten.

1. Ask students to tell some things they know about the number 10. Record their ideas on the board. (Use diagrams, graphs, pictures and symbols.)
2. Tell students that you are going to read *Moon To Sun* to learn more about the number 10.
3. After reading the story, have students cut out the ten pictures on Activity Sheet K-B to tell the story *Moon To Sun* as they listen to the story again. They can glue the pictures on 12″ by 18″ construction paper and use symbols to match the pictures. (1 + 1 + 1 + 1 + 1 + 1 + 1 + 1 + 1 + 1 = 10)
4. **Introduce the Problem**
   How can you use the pictures on Activity Sheet K-C to write a different addition story for 10?
5. **Materials**
   - Activity Sheet K-C (each pair of students)
   - 12″ by 18″ construction paper (each pair of students)
   - Glue
   - Scissors
   - Pencil
6. Students can work in pairs to write their own addition story for 10 using ten of the pictures on the paper.
7. **Instructions for Students**
   - Choose ten of the pictures.
   - Cut out the ten pictures and glue them on construction paper.
   - Use symbols to match the pictures and tell the addition story.

From the Classroom:
Kindergarten

Here, the student uses pictures to demonstrate he can write an addition story for ten. The task helps the student to see there are many ways to represent a given number and that a number does not change when the arrangement varies.

8. Have students evaluate their results in a class discussion. Each pair of students can share their addition story with the class to see how many different addition stories there were for 10.

Example:

2 cats		
2 frogs	3 frogs	
4 fish	4 fish	5 fish
1 turtle	2 roosters	3 frogs
1 rabbit	1 turtle	2 turtle
10	10	10

Talk about other ways to show the number 10 and look for patterns. Make an organized list.

cat	frog	fish	rooster	turtle	rabbit	total
2	2	4		1	1	10
	3	4	2	1		10
	3	5		2		10

9. Discuss the following questions with the class:

Discussion Questions: How Many Ways

- What can you tell about number 10?
- How many different ways can you write an addition story for 10?

10. Have students answer the questions in their journals.
★ *Encourage students to use diagrams, graphs, pictures and symbols to help answer the questions. You can have students dictate sentences to go with their representations.*
11. Use journal entries to assess students' ability to select an appropriate problem-solving strategy and describe it coherently. Students must be able to apply mathematical concepts to solve the problem. The emphasis here is more on the child's ability to communicate the process than on the *correct* answer.

From the Classroom: *Sample K–3*

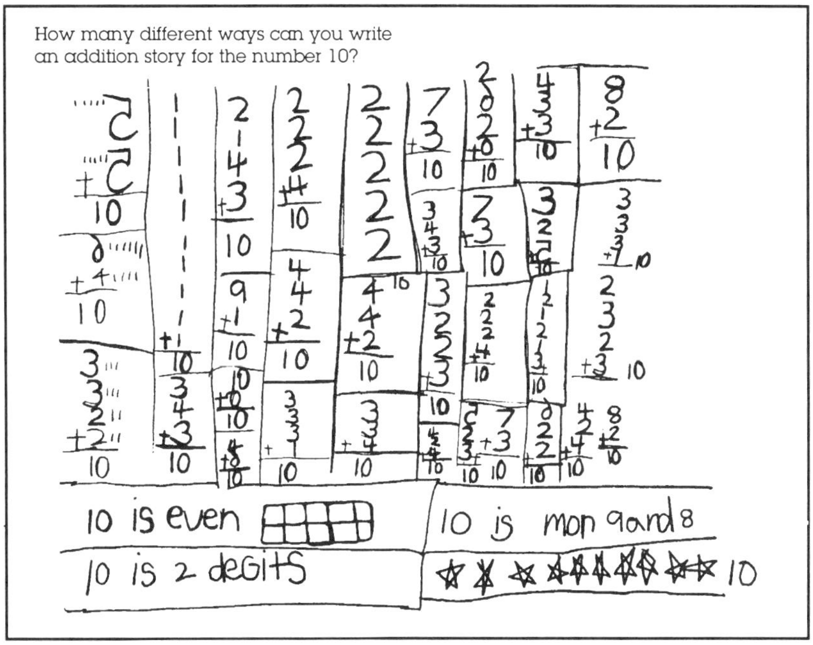

In this sample, the student shows an in-depth understanding of beginning number concepts. She demonstrates her knowledge of how numbers will not change if the arrangement varies. Her journal entry indicates an organized and coherent approach to the problem.

From the Classroom: *Sample K–4*

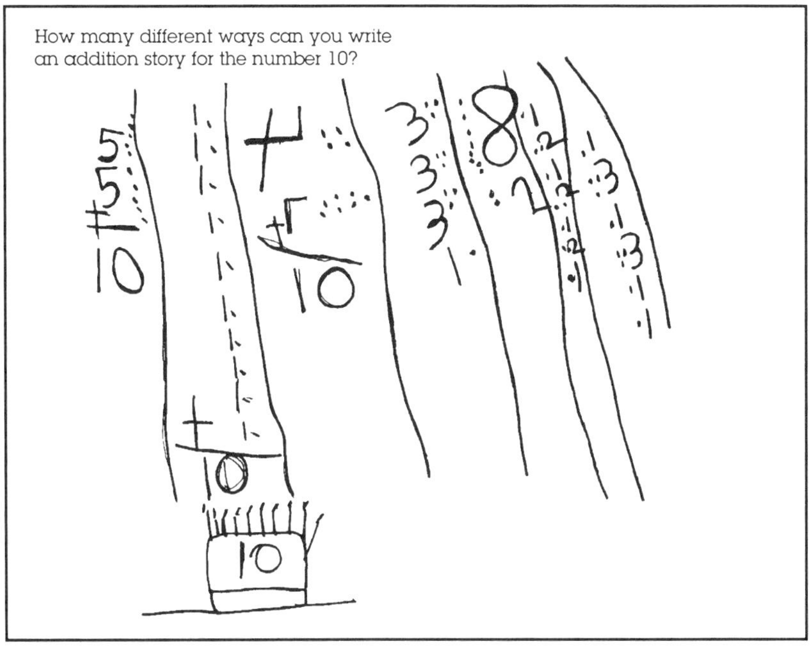

In this sample, the student is able to show some of the ways to write an addition story for 10. Although there is one error in computation, there are no apparent misunderstandings. He uses a concrete approach to solving the problem by drawing dots to represent each number before he computes his answer.

Picture Sheet One

Cut out the pictures. Make your own addition story.

moon

star

cloud

tree

hill

rooster

cat

house

boy

sun

Picture Sheet Two

Cut out the pictures and choose 10. Make your own addition story for 10.

cat

cat

frog

frog

frog

fish

fish

fish

fish

fish

rooster

rooster

turtle

turtle

rabbit

Questions For Reflection

1. At the end of the school year, pose the following questions:

Questions For Reflection
What I Learned About Numbers
• How do you use numbers each day?
• What did you learn about numbers?

Literature Connection: *One Watermelon Seed* by Celia Barker Lottridge
This counting book begins with one watermelon seed and ends with hundreds and thousands of popcorn puffs. Children count from one to ten and then to a hundred by ten.

2. Have students discuss the questions as a total group.
   Record their ideas on the board.
3. Tell students you are going to read another book about numbers.
   Ask them to listen carefully to see if there is anything more they can add to their list about numbers.
4. Read orally *One Watermelon Seed.*
5. After reading the story, discuss these questions:

Questions To Ask	Possible Answers
How did the numbers change in the story?	• First we counted by ones and then we counted by tens. • The numbers got bigger by one and then after 10, they got bigger by 10.
What did you learn in the story about numbers?	• There is a pattern when you count to 10 and when you count by tens to 100. • There were 10 more pumpkins than watermelons. • There were more corn seeds so there were more ears of corn than any other vegetable or fruit in the garden.
What do you still want to learn about numbers?	• How to count to 100. • How to tell what time it is when I have to go to school.

6. Review *Questions For Reflection* and add new ideas to the list on the board.
7. Have students answer the questions in their journals.
   ★ *Encourage students to use diagrams, graphs, pictures and symbols to help answer the questions. You can have students dictate sentences to go with their representations.*
8. Compare students' responses to their journal entry on *What I Already Know About Numbers.* You will gain information about:
   - whether they have expanded their knowledge of the numeration system and observed patterns.
   - their development of number sense.
   - how they use numbers in the real world.
   - whether they have increased their understanding of the concepts of whole number operations.
   - whether they have grown in their ability to express themselves in print.

- growth in their attitude towards mathematics.
- the effectiveness of your mathematics program.

9. Compare each students' response to *Questions for Reflection* at the beginning of the school year.

From the Classroom: *September*

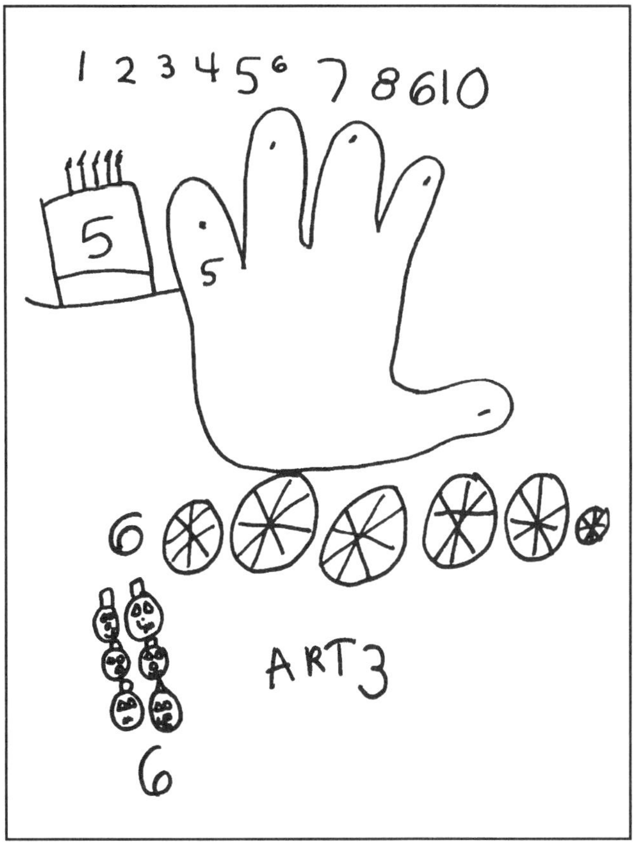

In September, the student uses numbers to count fingers on a hand, letters in a word and candles on a birthday cake.

From the Classroom: *June*

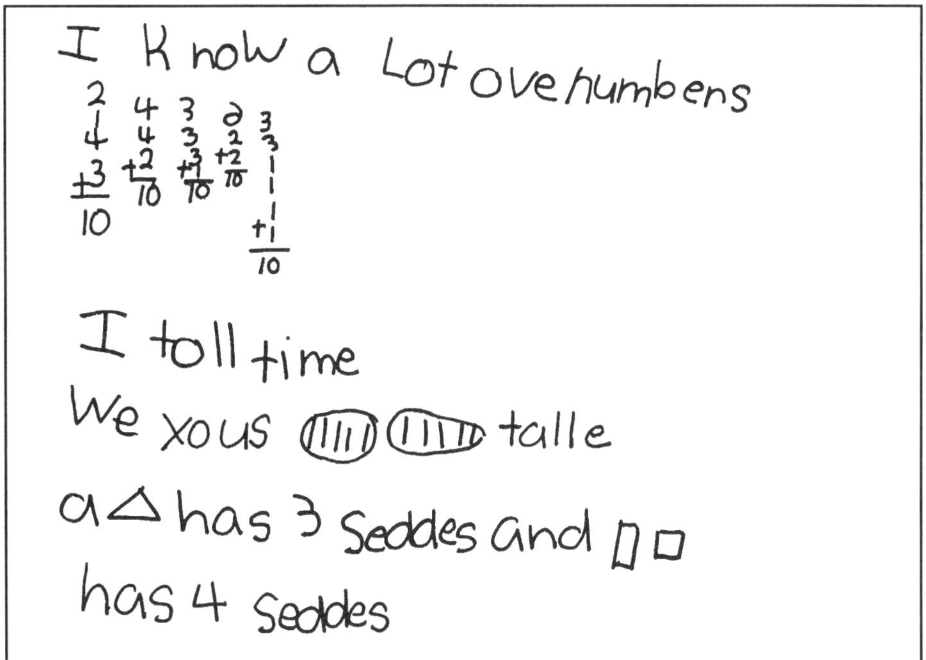

Translation: *I know a lot of numbers. I tell time. We use tally marks. A triangle has three sides and a rectangle and a square have 4 sides.*

In June, her view of numbers is expanded to move beyond counting to measuring time, identifying the number of sides on geometric shapes and recognizing a variety of number combinations to represent a given number. Her ability to express ideas in print has also grown.

Suggestions For Other Assessment Questions

Patterns

- Make a pattern with your unifix cubes. (or other materials, i.e., buttons)
- Tell about your pattern.

Measurement: Length

- How many unifix cubes long is your arm?
- Tell how you got your answer.

Measurement: Weight

- Name two things that are heavier than you.
- Explain how you know they are heavier than you.

Counting, Grouping and Place Value

- Tell how you counted the objects in the jar.
- Is there another way you could count the objects?

How Many Legs on 4 Cats?

- How did you solve the problem?
- Is there another way you could have solved the problem?

Probability and Statistics

- Tell what happened after you flipped a coin 10 times.
- What do you think will happen if you flip the coin 10 more times?

First Grade

Questions For Reflection
What I Already Know About Numbers
Literature Connection: *Ten Black Dots*

Math Exploration 1
Money
Literature Connection:: *Dollars and Cents For Harriet*

Math Exploration 2
How Many Feet? (Addition)
Literature Connection: *How Many Feet In The Bed?*

Questions For Reflection
What I Learned About Numbers
Literature Connection: *Demi's Count The Animals 1-2-3*

Suggestions For Other Assessment Questions

Questions For Reflection

Literature Connection: *Ten Black Dots* by Donald Crews
This counting book begins with one black dot that makes a sun and ends with ten black dots that make balloons stuck in a tree.

1. At the beginning of the school year, pose the following questions:

Questions For Reflection
What I Already Know About Numbers
• How do you use numbers each day?
• What do you know about numbers?
• What do you want to learn about numbers?

2. Have students discuss the questions as a total group. Record their ideas on the board.
3. Tell students that you are going to read a story about numbers. Ask them to listen carefully to see if there is anything they can add to their list about what they know about numbers.
4. Read orally: *Ten Black Dots.*
5. After reading the story, discuss these questions:

Questions To Ask	Possible Answers
How were numbers used in the story?	• To show 2 black dots. • To show numbers from one to ten with black dots.
How can you find out how many dots are on a page?	• Look at the number. • Count the dots.
What does the graph tell you?	• Two is one more than one. • Ten is the biggest number. • Seven is two less than nine.
What can you tell us about the number 4?	• $2 + 2 = 4$ • $1 + 1 + 1 + 1 = 4$ • 4 is an even number. • 4 is one more than 3
How can you change a number?	• Add one dot to four and you have five dots. $(4 + 1 = 5)$ • Take away two dots from eight and you have six dots. $(8 - 2 = 6)$
We talked about how the book used numbers. How do you use numbers each day? *(Encourage students to be specific.)*	• To tell my age. • To tell what time I have to be at school. • To count how many books I have on my shelf. • To see how much I weigh.
What do you know about numbers?	• I can count 5 objects by counting: 1, 2, 3, 4, 5. • I can count to 10 by twos: 2, 4, 6, 8, 10 • $2 + 2 = 4$ and $3 + 1 = 4$
What do you want to learn about numbers?	• How to count to 100. • How to count the money in my bank.

6. Review *Questions For Reflection* and add new ideas to the list on the board.
7. Write a class journal entry modeling how to answer the questions. Discuss how this is just one way to answer the questions. Students can share other ways.
8. Have students answer the questions in their journals.
   ★ *Encourage students to use diagrams, graphs, pictures and symbols to help explain their answers. You can have students dictate sentences to go with their representations.*
9. The journal entries will give you information about:
   - students' understanding of the numeration system.
   - their number sense.
   - how they use numbers in the real world.
   - their understanding of the concepts of whole number operations.
   - how they select and use computation to solve problems.
   - their attitude towards mathematics.
10. Save the journal entries and use them to compare each student's response to *Questions For Reflection* at the end of the school year. (See *From the Classroom,* page 42).
11. **Optional:** Students can write their own class big book: *Ten Green Dots.*

Math Exploration 1: Money

Literature Connection: *Dollars and Cents for Harriet* by Betsy and Giulio Maestro
Harriet needs five dollars to buy something she wants at the toy store and learns different ways to add coins to make a dollar as she earns the money.

1. Tell students they will be studying money. Ask these questions:
   - Why do we need money?
   - What do you already know about money?
   - What do you want to learn about money?
2. Remind students to listen carefully as you read, *Dollars and Cents for Harriet* so that you can discuss how money is used in the story.
3. After reading the story, discuss these questions:

Questions To Ask	Possible Answers
What was the problem in the story?	• Harriet had a dollar and she needed four more dollars to buy a new kite.
What did Harriet have to know about money to solve this problem?	• She needed 4 more dollars because \$1.00 + \$4.00 = \$5.00 *or* \$5.00 – \$1.00 = \$4.00. • 100 pennies = \$1.00 • You count nickels by five's because a nickel is worth 5¢.
What did you learn from this story about money?	• There are different ways to make \$1.00. • 20 nickels = \$1.00.

4. During the unit on money, provide these hands-on opportunities:
   - Identify and describe a penny, nickel and dime. (How they look, size, color, shape, value) Provide students with a magnifier to closely examine coins and have them report their discoveries orally or in writing.
   - Play *Mystery Bag* with the students. Have one student place a coin in a bag and then describe it to other students until they can correctly name the hidden coin.
   - Compare a penny, nickel and dime to find out how they are alike and different. then have students use Activity Sheet 1-A to create Venn diagrams and compare two coins, as illustrated below:

From the Classroom: *Sample 1–1*

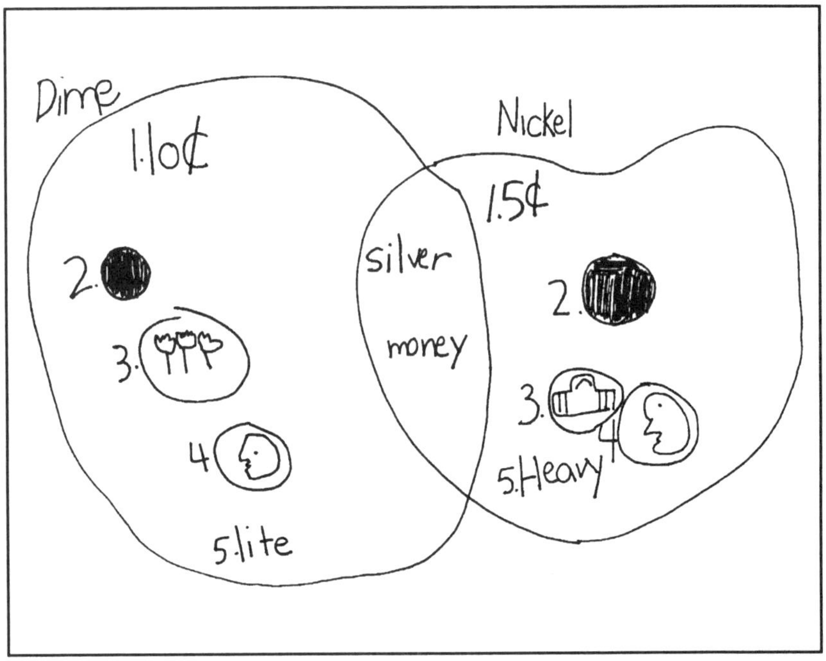

In Samples 1–1 and 1–2, two students demonstrate their ability to make comparisons and show how two coins are alike and different. Although the first sample has more pictures than words, the ideas in each sample are communicated effectively. The task requires the students to share their ideas in an organized manner using a Venn diagram.

From the Classroom: *Sample 1–2*

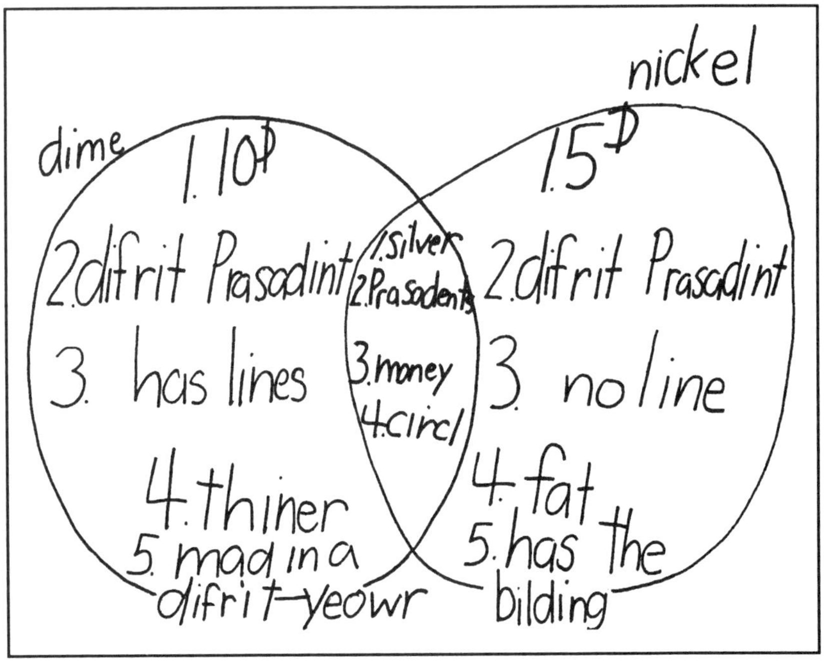

- Count coins that are the same to find the value. Discuss different strategies for counting the coins.

- Count coins to find the value. Discuss different strategies for counting the coins.

- List all the ways to make a given amount. Example: 11¢

dimes	nickels	pennies
1		1
	2	1
		11

- Make a graph using real coins to show how many pennies, nickels and dimes are in a toy bank. Count to find the value using the graph. Then show students another way to represent the data by making a bar graph:

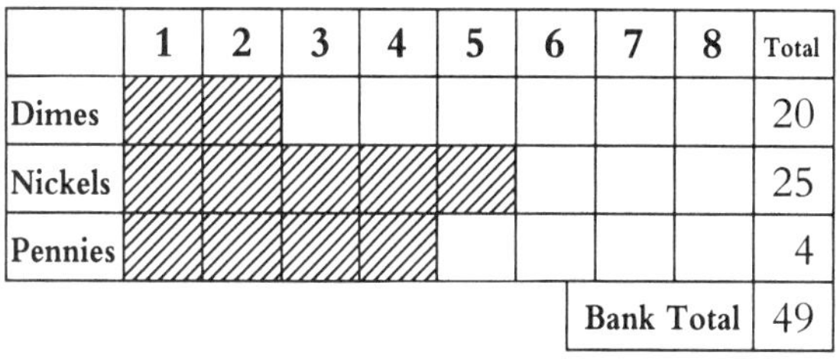

(Use Activity Sheet 1-B for more practice.)
Students can come up with other ways to represent the data that will help them find the value of the coins in a toy bank.

5. When a unit on money is complete, pose the following questions about money:

Discussion Questions: Money

- Tell about a penny, nickel and dime. (How they look, size, color, shape, value, etc.)
- How many different ways can you make 23 cents to buy a pencil at the store?
- Do you think you are good at counting money?
- What else did you learn that will help you count money?

6. Have students answer the questions in their journals.
★ Encourage students to use diagrams, charts, pictures and symbols to explain their answers. You can have students dictate sentences to go with their representations.
7. Use journal entries to assess students' level of understanding of money and their ability to express what they know. The following examples demonstrate a range of student responses that is likely to occur in your classroom.

A penney is round andsmall and brownish and copper and one cent. A nickel is big and Silver It is werth five cents. And rond. A dime is very small and rownd and silver and werth ten cents becase it is the smallest dusent meen its less its still ten cents.

page 1

I learned a Quoter is 25¢

I learned Four Quarters are in a dolen.

I learned a nickel is 5¢

I learned twenty nickel mak a dolen.

I learned 100 penneys mak a dolen.

I learned a Quorter and a dime has lines And a nickel and penney has no lines.

Im great at coting money.

I learned how to play stor.

page 2

From the Classroom: *Sample 1–3*

In this sample, the student demonstrates a complete grasp of the concept of money. His answers to the discussion questions are communicated effectively. He uses sophisticated strategies to count money and seems to fully understand that a given amount of money can be represented in a variety of ways.

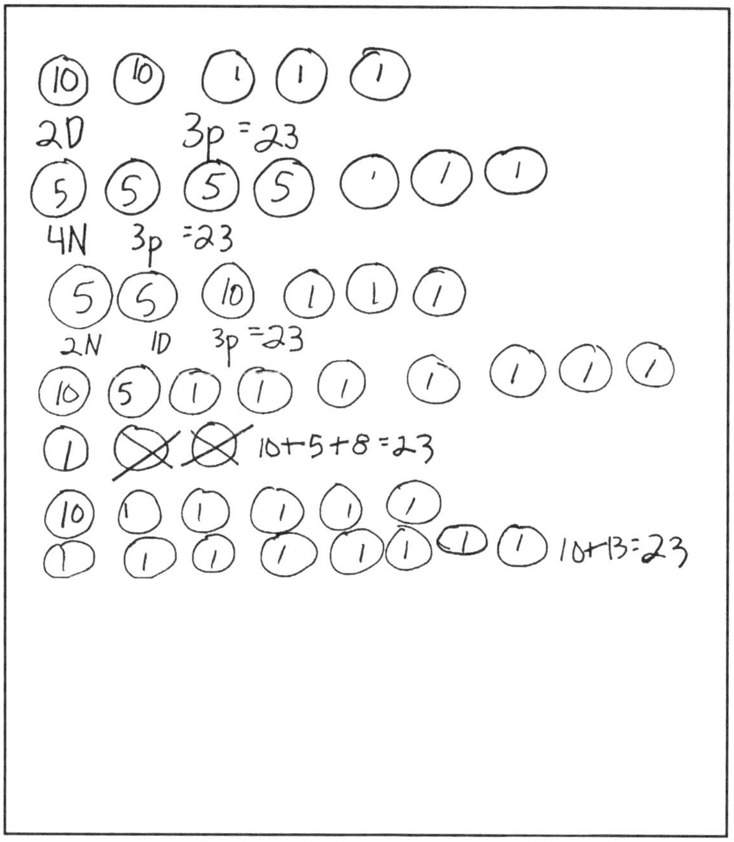

page 3

From the Classroom: *Sample 1–4*

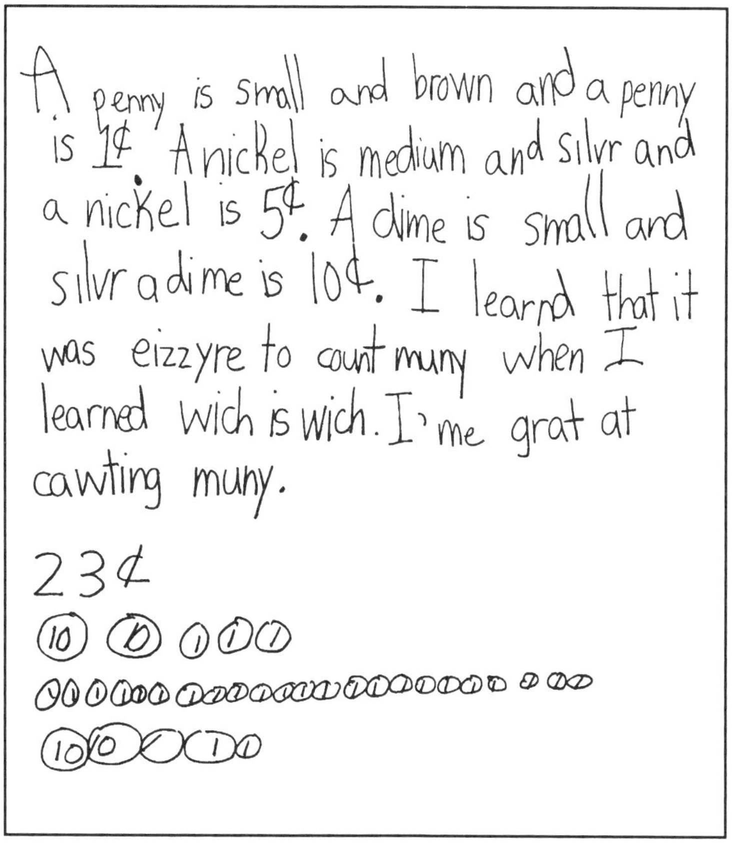

In this sample, the student answers all questions satisfactorily but not as completely as sample 1–3. She only shows three ways to represent 23 cents and two examples were the same.

Name ______________________

Venn Diagram

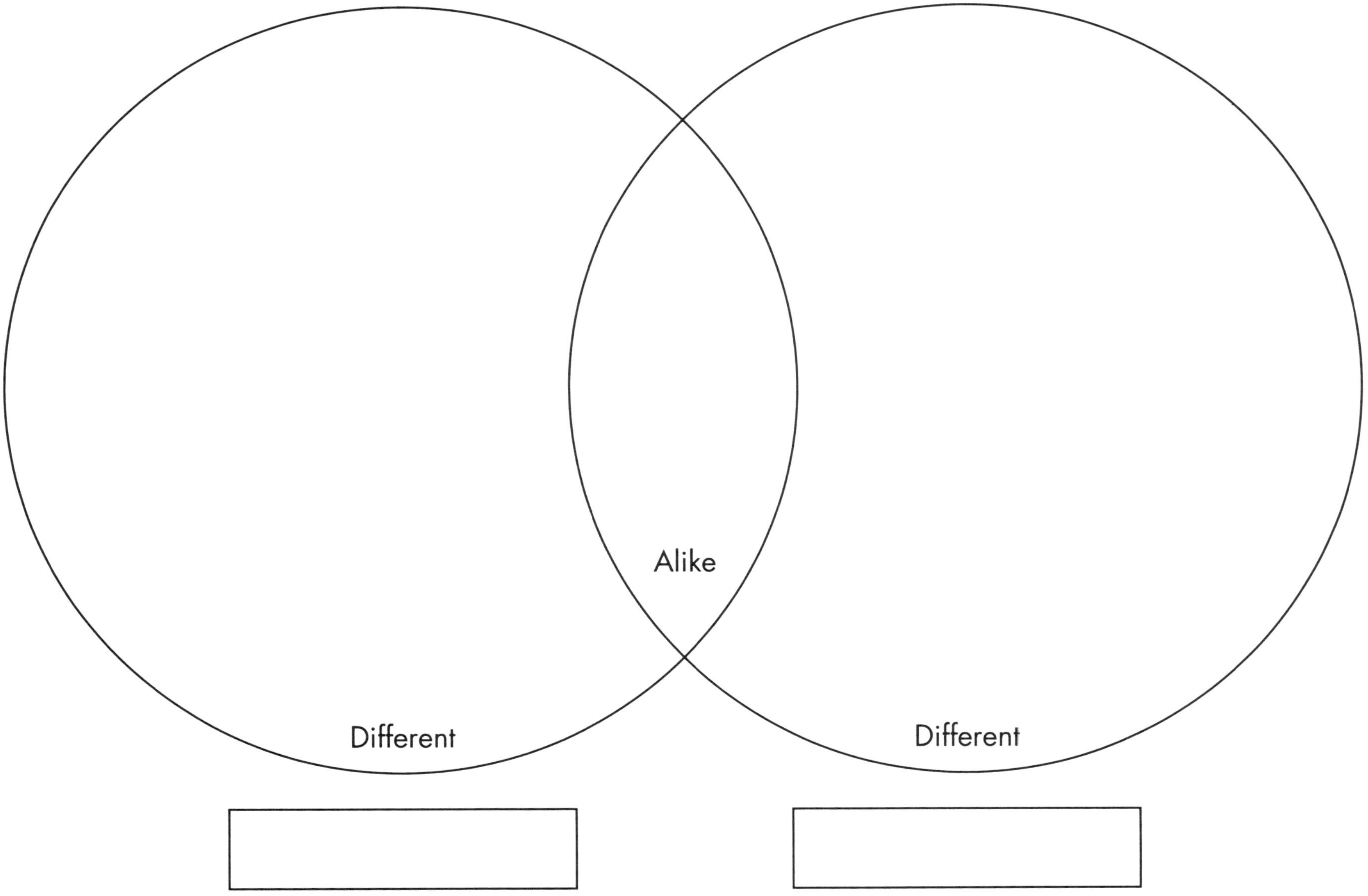

How Much Money?

	Dimes	Nickels	Pennies
1			
2			
3			
4			
5			
6			
7			
8			
9			
10			
Total			

Total Dimes	
Total Pennies	
Total Nickels	
Bank Total	

Name ______________________________

Math Exploration 2: How Many Feet? *(Addition)*

Literature Connection: *How Many Feet in the Bed?* by Diane Johnston Hamm
In this story, a family of five count their feet as they move in and out of bed early one morning.

1. Read orally *How Many Feet In The Bed?*
2. Have students act out the story to count how many feet in the bed.
3. Make a chart to show how many feet in the bed:

People	Feet
0	0
1	2
2	4
3	6
4	8
5	10

Ask these questions:
- If 8 feet, how many people?
- If 12 feet, how many people?

4. Discuss and record other strategies for counting how many feet in the bed; use objects, draw pictures, etc.
5. Students can work in pairs. Provide objects, calculators, paper and pencils for each pair of students. Ask them to find out:
   - How many feet at their tables?
   - How many feet at two tables?
   - How many feet in the classroom?

   ★ *Have students make an estimate first before answering each question. Students need to show their work and be able to share the strategies used to solve each problem.*
6. Discuss all the strategies used to solve each problem as a total group.
7. Make a class list to show: *How Many Feet?*

2 Feet	4 Feet	6 Feet	8 Feet	10 Feet
person	dog	ant	spider	crab
duck	horse	cricket	octopus	squid
chicken	cat	grasshopper		
bird	elephant			

8. Ask these questions and discuss strategies used to solve each problem:
   - How many feet on 3 horses?
   - How many feet on 2 spiders?
   - How many feet on 2 chickens and 2 cows?
9. Students can write their own questions using the chart.

10. **Introduce the Problem**
The little girl found her 3 cats and 4 dogs in the bed. If she jumped in the bed with her pet spider, how many feet in the bed?
11. **Materials**
    - Activity Sheet 1-C
    - Objects
    - Calculators
    - Pencil
12. Students can work in pairs to solve the problem.
13. **Instructions for Students**
    - Read the problem carefully and discuss. (This can be teacher directed.)
    - Write an estimate.
    - Choose a strategy to help solve the problem.
    - Carry out the plan.
    - Show your work and record your answer on the activity sheet.
    - Check your answer to make sure it makes sense.
14. Students evaluate their results in a class discussion by sharing how they solved the problem.
15. Discuss the following questions with the class:

Discussion Question: How Many Feet?

- Describe the problem in your own words.
- How did you solve the problem?
- Is there another way you could have solved the problem?
- How many feet and tails are there altogether in the bed?
- What mathematics did you use?
- How did you feel about the problem?

16. Have students answer the questions in their journals.
★ Encourage students to use diagrams, graphs, pictures and symbols to help answer the questions. You can have students dictate sentences to go with their representations. Students can glue the activity sheet in their journals to help explain how they solved the problem.
17. Use journal entries to assess students' ability to select an appropriate problem-solving strategy and describe it coherently. Students must be able to apply mathematical concepts to solve the problem. The emphasis here is more on the child's ability to communicate the process than on the correct answer.

page 1

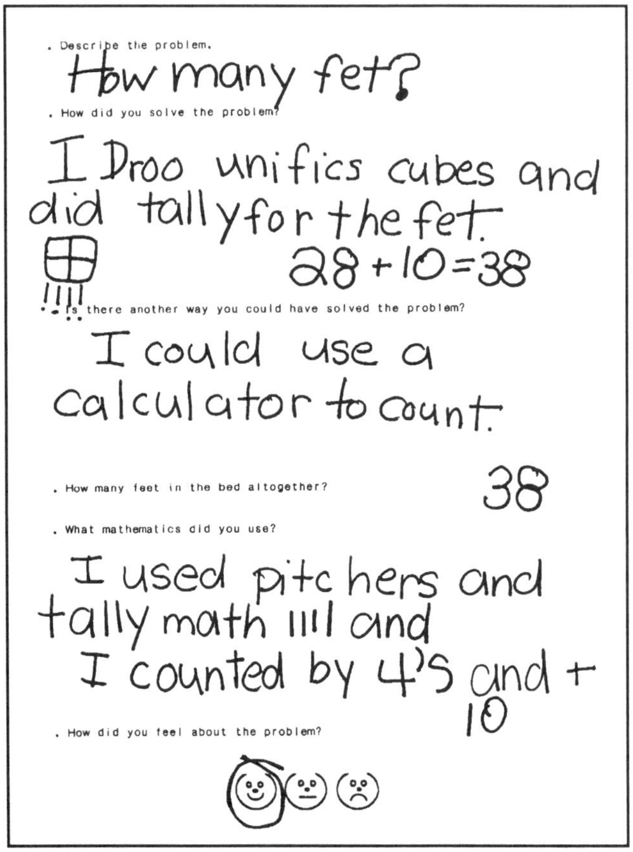
. Describe the problem.

How many fet?

. How did you solve the problem?

I Droo unifics cubes and did tally for the fet.

28+10=38

. Is there another way you could have solved the problem?

I could use a calculator to count.

. How many feet in the bed altogether? 38

. What mathematics did you use?

I used pitchers and tally math IIII and I counted by 4's and + 10

. How did you feel about the problem?

page 2

From the Classroom: *Sample 1–5*

In this sample, the student solves the problem successfully using a concrete method. Then she finds another way to solve the problem using a sophisticated equation. Her journal entry indicates an organized and coherent approach to the problem.

From the Classroom: *Sample 1–6*

In this sample, the student demonstrates that he can solve the problem accurately. However, all questions are not answered and there are some gaps in his attempt to explain the strategies he used to approach it. He uses pictures to solve the problem but does not explain how he counted the pictures. The answer is correct on his activity sheet; however, the answer in his journal entry does not match.

page 1

. Describe the problem.

. How did you solve the problem?

I made pictures

How did you count?

. Is there another way you could have solved the problem?

unifix

. How many feet in the bed altogether?

. What mathematics did you use?

3

canwt by wons

ones

. How did you feel about the problem?

page 2

Name ____________________

Problem:

The little girl found her 3 cats and 4 dogs in the bed.
If she jumped in the bed with her pet spider, how many feet in the bed?

Estimate: [ ]   Answer: [ ]

Show your work:

Questions for Reflection

Literature Connection: *Demi's Count the Animals 1-2-3*
This counting book begins with one rhino and ends with one hundred animals. Children count from one to twenty and then to one hundred by two and five. Each number is introduced with rhyme.

1. At the end of the year, pose the following questions:

Questions For Reflection
What I Learned About Numbers
• How do you use numbers each day? • What did you learn about numbers? • What do you still want to learn about numbers?

2. Have students discuss the questions as a total group. Record their ideas on the board.
3. Tell students you are going to read another book about numbers. Ask them to listen carefully to see if there is anything more they can add to their list about numbers.
4. Read orally: *Demi's Count the Animals 1-2-3.*
5. After reading the story, discuss these questions:

Questions To Ask	Possible Answers
What did you learn in the story about numbers?	• It is easier to count the 100 animals when you group them by 10. • 20 + 20 = 40 because 2 + 2 = 4 and you just add a zero. • 14 rabbits + 14 snowflakes = 28 because 10+ 10 = 20 and 4 + 4 = 8 and 20 + 8 = 28.
What do you still want to learn about numbers?	• How to answer problems like 4 x 5. • How to count faster. • How to measure long things using a meter stick.

6. Review *Questions for Reflection* and add new ideas to the list on the board.
7. Have students write in their journals.
   ★ *Encourage students to use diagrams, graphs, pictures and symbols to help explain their answers.*
8. Compare students' responses to their journal entry on *What I Already Know About Numbers.* You will gain information about:
   - whether they have expanded their knowledge of the numeration system and observed patterns.
   - their development of number sense.
   - how they use numbers in the real world.
   - whether they have increased their understanding of the concepts of whole number operations.
   - whether they have grown in their ability to express themselves in print.
   - how they select and use computation to solve problems.
   - growth in their attitude towards mathematics.
   - the effectiveness of your mathematics program.
9. Compare each student's response to *Questions For Reflection* at the beginning of the school year.

From the Classroom: *September*

How do you use numbers each day?

on a
clock car
on a

In September, the student uses numbers to write on a paper and to tell time.

From the Classroom: *June*

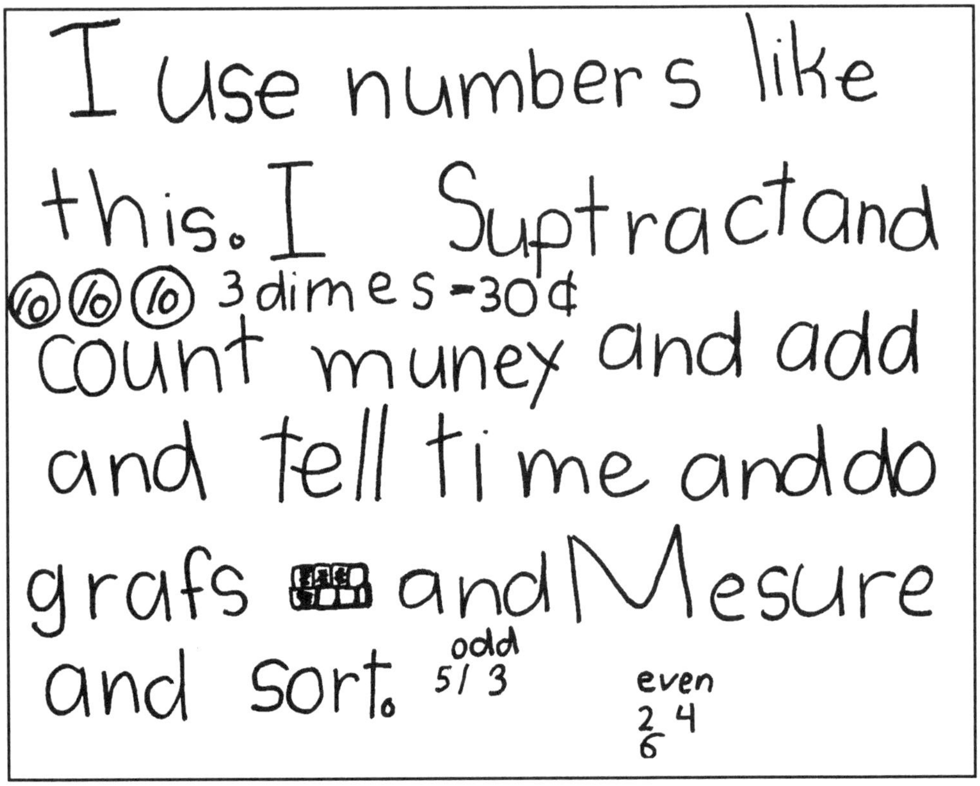
I use numbers like
this. I Suptractand
3 dimes -30¢
count muney and add
and tell time anddo
grafs and Mesure
and sort. odd 5 1 3 even 2 4 6

In June, his view of numbers is expanded to a variety of daily life experiences such as counting money, recording data on a graph, measuring and sorting objects. He observes the pattern in odd and even numbers and his ability to express his ideas in print has grown.

Suggestions For Other Assessment Questions

Patterns
- Make a pattern using pattern blocks. (and other materials)
- Tell about your pattern.

Measurement: Length
- How many unifix cubes long are you?
- Tell how you got your answer.

How Many Ways? *(Discrete Mathematics)*
- How many different ways can you write an addition story for 12?
- Tell about the number 12.

What I Already Know About Subtraction
- How do we use subtraction each day?
- Write your own subtraction problem for 12 – 5 and tell how you solved the problem.
- How can addition help you with subtraction?

Tangrams *(Geometry)*
- Tell about the different tangram shapes.
- What are some ways that you could sort your shapes?
- How many different shapes can you make using 2 or 3 tangram pieces?
- Tell about the shapes that you made.

Graph Interpretation
- What does the graph tell you?
- What comparisons can you make?

Second Grade

Questions For Reflection
What I Already Know About Numbers
Literature Connection: *10 For Dinner*

Math Exploration 1
Measurement: Length
Literature Connection: *Jim & the Beanstalk*

Math Exploration 2
More Than, Less Than or Twice As Many? (Algebra)
Literature Connection: *The Baby Blue Cat & the Whole Batch of Cookies*

Questions For Reflection
What I Learned About Numbers
Literature Connection: *Two Ways to Count to Ten*

Suggestions For Other Assessment Questions

Questions For Reflection

Literature Connection: *10 For Dinner* by Jo Ellen Bogart
Margo invites ten friends to her birthday. The book explores different combinations for ten as details of the party are described.

1. At the beginning of the school year, pose the following questions:

Questions For Reflection
What I Already Know About Numbers
• How do you use numbers each day?
• What are some things you already know about numbers?
• What are some things you want to learn about numbers?

2. Have students discuss the questions as a total group. Record their ideas on the board.
3. Tell students that you are going to read a story about numbers. Ask them to listen carefully to see if there is anything they can add to their list about what they already know about numbers.
4. Read orally *10 for Dinner.*
5. After reading the story, discuss these questions:

Questions To Ask	Possible Answers
How were numbers used in the story?	• To tell what time children came to the party. • To count the guests at the party. • To count how many guests wore shorts, dresses, jeans, jogging suits or costumes.
How do you use numbers each day? *(Encourage students to be specific.)*	• To count money in my wallet. • Add how many green and red candies are in a bag. • To count candles on a birthday cake.
What are some things you already know about numbers? *(Encourage students to give examples using diagrams, graphs, pictures, charts or symbols.)*	• 2, 4, 6, 8 and 10 are even numbers because you can divide each number in half equally. • 24 is greater than 12 because 2 tens and 4 ones is more than 1 ten and 2 ones. • There are different ways to name the number 10: $5+5=10$ *or* $(6+3)+1=10$.
What are some things you want to learn about numbers?	• How to add big numbers like $248+157$. • How to make change for a $1.00 if you buy a box of crayons that costs 79¢ and you give the clerk a dollar bill. • How to tell time so you know when to go to recess and lunch.

6. Review the *Questions for Reflection* and add new ideas to their list on the board.
7. Write a class journal entry modeling how to answer the questions, if necessary. Discuss how this is just one way to answer the questions. Students can share other ways.
8. Have students answer the questions in their journals.
   ★ *Encourage students to use diagrams, graphs, pictures and symbols to help explain their answers.*

9. The journal entries will give you information about:
   - students' understanding of the numeration system.
   - their number sense.
   - how they use numbers in the real world.
   - their understanding of the concepts of whole number operations.
   - how they select and use computation to solve problems.
   - their attitude towards mathematics.
10. Save the journal entries and use them to compare each student's response to *Questions for Reflection* at the end of the school year. (See *From the Classroom,* page 58).

Math Exploration 1: Measurement – Length

Literature Connection: *Jim & the Beanstalk* by Raymond Briggs
After Jim decides to climb to the top of a large plant growing outside his window, he finds a castle owned by a giant who has some problems. Jim helps the giant solve the problems by using a measuring tape to help him get glasses and a new set of teeth.

1. Tell students they will be studying measurement. Ask these questions:
   - What is measurement?
   - How do we use measurement in our daily lives?
2. Remind students to listen carefully as you read *Jim & the Beanstalk* so that they can discuss how measurement is used in the story.
3. After reading the story, discuss these questions:

Questions To Ask	Possible Answers
How did measurement help Jim solve the Giant's problems?	• He used a tape to measure the Giant's head for glasses. • He used a tape to measure the Giant's mouth for teeth.
How could Jim solve the Giant's problems if he didn't have a tape measure?	• Allow students to be creative with their answers. *(Stressing the need for standard units of measurement)*
What is important to remember when measuring something?	• You need to line your measurement tool up very carefully. • You need to count carefully to be as accurate as possible.
What did you learn from this story about measurement?	• You need a standard unit of measurement. • Measurement can help solve problems in our daily lives. • An oculist uses measurement to make glasses.

4. During the unit on measurement, provide these hands on opportunities:
   - Students make comparisons between objects using various objects in the room. Encourage students to use words such as *longer, shorter* and *length* when comparing objects.
   - Students sort and order various objects in the room by size.
   - Have students compare objects using a variety of nonstandard units such as paper clips, unifix cubes and toothpicks. Encourage students to make an estimate before measuring. Students can discuss what happens when they measure the same object using a different nonstandard unit each time. (The bigger the non-standard unit the smaller the number of units used.) This will help them to see the need for standard units of measurement.
   - Students compare objects using standard units (customary and metric). Encourage students to make an estimate before measuring. They can use calculators to find the difference between their estimate and the measurement. This will help them to make more reasonable estimates.
   - Students select the appropriate standard unit of measurement given an object to measure.
   - Students measure the distance around their table to find the perimeter.
5. When the unit on measurement–length is complete, pose the following discussion questions about measurement.

Discussion Questions: Measurement–Length

- What is measurement?
- How do we use measurement in our daily lives?
- Name two things that are taller than you and two things that are shorter than you.
- Why do we need standard units of measurement?
- What would be the best tool to measure the length of:
  your finger?
  a book?
  a person?
  the room?
  Explain why you chose each tool.
- What is important to remember when measuring the length of your finger, a book, the room, a person?

6. Have students answer the questions in their journals.
   ★ *Encourage students to use diagrams, charts, pictures and symbols to help explain their answers.*
7. Use journal entries to assess students' level of understanding of measurement and their ability to express what they know. The following examples demonstrate a range of student responses that is likely to occur in your classroom.

From the Classroom: *Sample 2–1*

In this sample, the student displays an understanding of the concept of measurement. All discussion questions were answered successfully but some questions could have been answered more completely. For example, he does not fully explain why you need to mark your place when measuring. He seems to recognize the need for standard units of measurement in everyday situations.

Measurement Nov. 12, 1992

1. Measurment is when you have some thing like a ruler, cubes, rods, a string, tape to measure to see how long it is or seeing if things fit.
2. We use measurment every day to see how tall you are and to find out how long and short things are. Other kinds of measuement are cooking with a measuring cup and seeing how much you weigh. (Right!)
3. my mom and dad are taller then me be cause they are grown up and I live with them and see them everyday.
4. My two frends are shorter then me because I have stood up to them before and I found out they are shorter then me.
5. I would use cubes to measure my finger because they are small and rods for a book and strings for a person and a room because they are biger
6. It is important to use the same objects because some objects are bigger then others we need feet or inches so you get the same anser.
7. The most important thing to remember when your measuring is to mark your place. You alwise (always) need good measurements to make somthing pirfect (Why is that important?)

From the Classroom: *Sample 2–2*

In this sample, the student also displays an understanding of the concept of measurement but all questions are not answered and ideas need further explanation. Although there are no apparent misunderstandings, some important ideas are not clearly stated. The need for standard units of measurement was not effectively communicated.

Meausurement Nov 12, 92

1. Measurement is How long on short, it is
2. My Dad and The car are Big My Babe sester is smal
3. finger cubes book rods person string room cubes (Why will you use these tools?)
4. you yus The Sam uNit beckus if you yus a diffit unit then you well not get the same number
5. You yus the sam unit and put yur finger in the spas at the ened

Good!

Math Exploration 2:
More Than, Less Than or Twice As Many? *(Algebra)*

Literature Connection:

The Baby Blue Cat and the Whole Batch of Cookies by Ainslie Pryor

After Baby Blue Cat sneaks in the kitchen and finishes all the cookies that Mama baked for her four baby cats to eat after playtime, he worries how he will tell her what he has done.

1. Read orally *The Baby Blue Cat and the Whole Batch Of Cookies.*
2. After reading the story, ask this question:
   If the baby cat had a bag of 9 cookies and there were twice as many chocolate as vanilla cookies in the bag, how many chocolate and vanilla cookies were in the bag?
3. Have students discuss the problem, make an estimate and brainstorm different strategies that can be used to solve the problem. (Use objects, draw picture, make a chart.)
4. Solve the problem as a total group and share different strategies used:

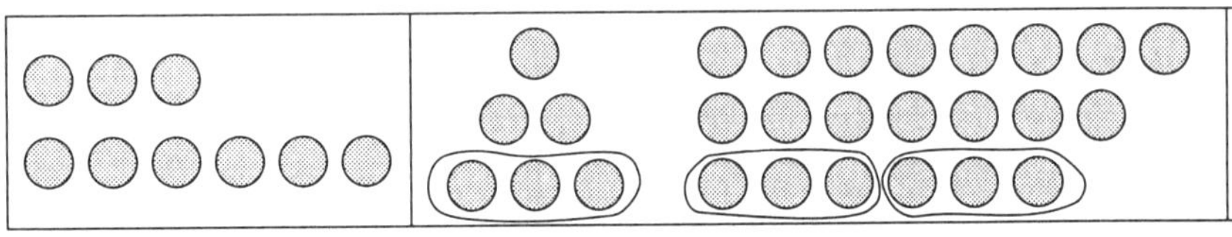

1 + 8
2 + 9
3 + 6

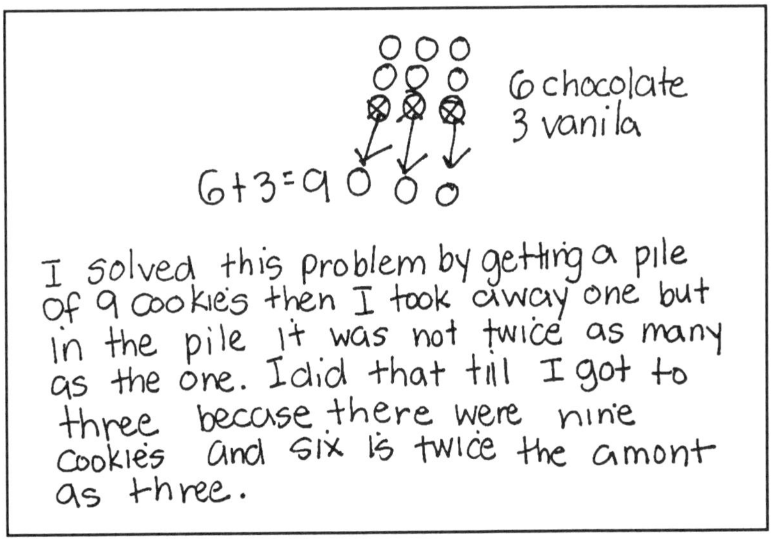

6 chocolate
3 vanila
6+3=9

I solved this problem by getting a pile of 9 cookies then I took away one but in the pile it was not twice as many as the one. I did that till I got to three becase there were nine cookies and six is twice the amont as three.

From the Classroom: *Sample 2–3*

In both samples 2–3 and 2–4, the students are able to solve the problems and explain their solutions. The tasks require them to choose a strategy and justify their mathematical thinking. They help students see that there is more than one way to solve a problem.

5. Here is another practice question to solve as a total group: If the baby cat had a bag of 7 cookies and there were 3 more chocolate than vanilla, how many chocolate and vanilla cookies were in the bag?

From the Classroom: *Sample 2–4*

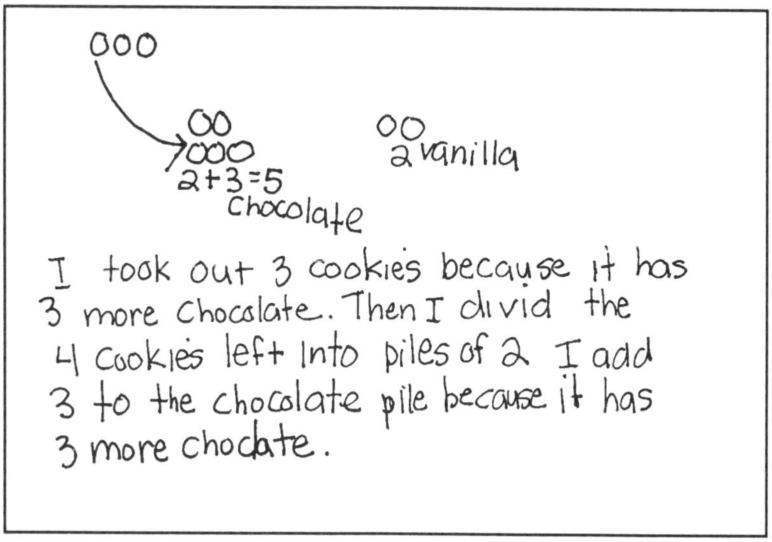

6. **Introduce the Problem**
The mother cat baked cookies and placed them in 4 bags. She put chocolate and vanilla cookies in each bag. Bag One has 12 cookies, Bag Two has 19 cookies, Bag Three has 24 cookies and Bag Four has 3 dozen cookies. Then she told the baby cat he could have all the cookies if he told her how many chocolate and vanilla cookies were in each bag. These were the 4 clues that the mother cat gave the baby cat to help him:

1. Bag One has twice as many chocolate as vanilla.
2. Bag Two has 3 less vanilla than chocolate.
3. Bag Three has 2 more vanilla than chocolate.
4. Bag Four has 4 less chocolate than vanilla.

How many chocolate and vanilla cookies are in each bag?

7. **Materials**
   - Student Activity Sheet 2-A. (one for each group of students)
   - Student Activity Sheet 2-B. (one for each student)
   - Objects to represent cookies. (Each group will need 40.)
   - Pencil
   - Brown and yellow crayon (optional)
8. Students can work in groups of three. Each person has a job: *Counter, Mover* and *Checker.* The *Counter* counts the objects, the *Mover* moves the objects as other members of the group offer suggestions, and the *Checker* makes sure the answer meets the conditions of the problem. All students are responsible to share their solutions so they need to actively participate in the group process.
9. **Instructions for Students**
   - Read the problem carefully and discuss.
   - Write an estimate for each bag.
   - Choose a strategy to help solve the problem.
   - Count out the number of cookies in each bag using objects. (Counter)
   - Use the objects to represent the cookies. (Mover)
   - Record your answers on the activity sheet.
   - Check answers to make sure they make sense. (Checker)
10. Have students share their solutions to the problem and the strategies they used.
11. Discuss the following questions with the class:

Discussion Questions: More Than, Less Than, or Twice as Many?

- What was the problem?
- How did you solve each clue?
- Is there another way you could have solved each clue?
- How many chocolate and vanilla cookies are in each bag?
- What mathematics did you use?
- How did you feel about the problem? Why?

12. Have students answer the questions in their journals.
    ★ Encourage students to use diagrams, charts, pictures and symbols to help explain their answers. Students can cut up Activity Sheet 2-B and glue in their journals to help explain how they solved each of the 4 clues.
13. Use journal entries to assess students' ability to select an appropriate problem-solving strategy and describe it coherently. Students must be able to apply mathematical concepts to solve the problem. The emphasis here is more on the child's ability to communicate the process than on the correct answer.
14. ***Answer Key:***

Bag One:	8 Chocolate	4 Vanilla
Bag Two:	11 Chocolate	8 Vanilla
Bag Three:	11 Chocolate	13 Vanilla
Bag Four:	16 Chocolate	20 Vanilla

From the Classroom: *Sample 2–4*

In this sample, the student demonstrates a thorough understanding of the concept of a variable and primary grade algebraic operations. All questions are communicated clearly and effectively. Her strategies are sophisticated and she is able to describe more than one solution to each clue.

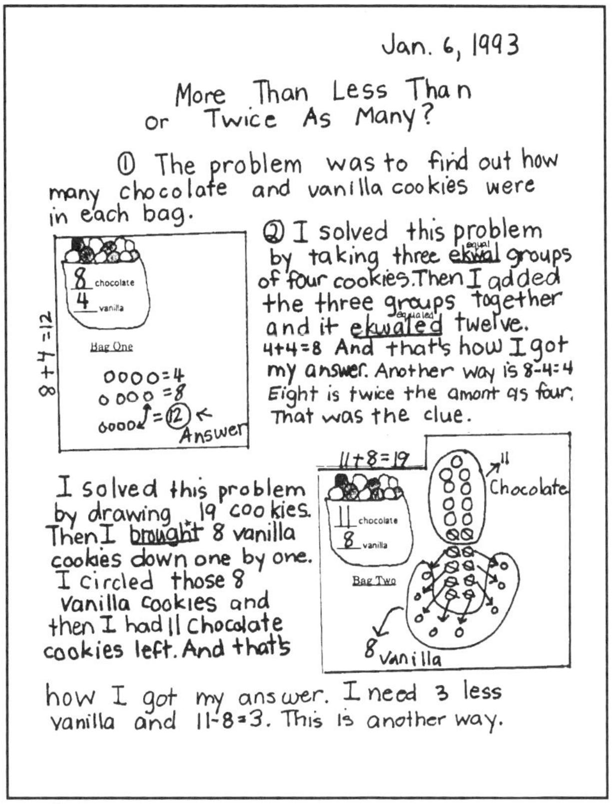

Jan. 6, 1993

More Than Less Than or Twice As Many?

① The problem was to find out how many chocolate and vanilla cookies were in each bag.

② I solved this problem by taking three ekwal (equal) groups of four cookies. Then I added the three groups together and it ekwaled (equaled) twelve. 4+4=8 And that's how I got my answer. Another way is 8-4=4 Eight is twice the amont as four. That was the clue.

I solved this problem by drawing 19 cookies. Then I brought 8 vanilla cookies down one by one. I circled those 8 vanilla cookies and then I had 11 chocolate cookies left. And that's how I got my answer. I need 3 less vanilla and 11-8=3. This is another way.

page 1

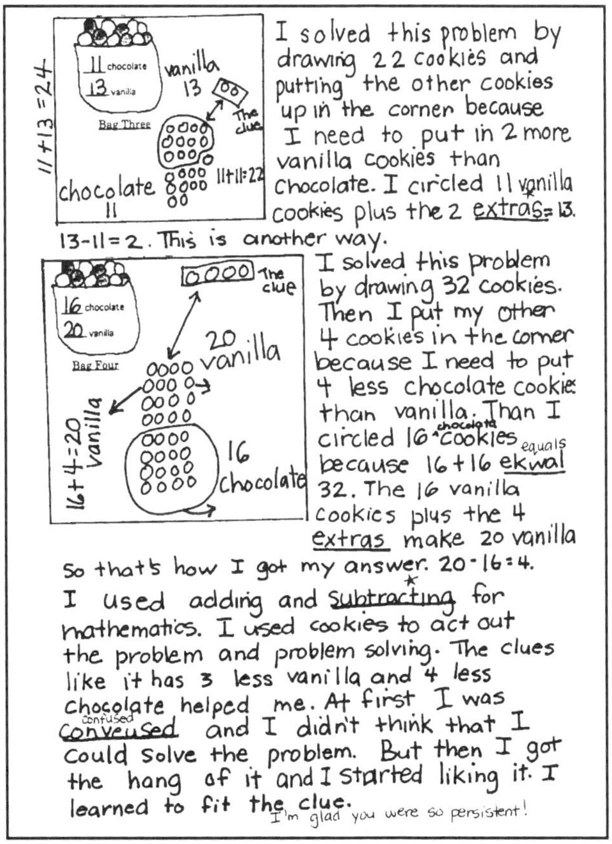

I solved this problem by drawing 22 cookies and putting the other cookies up in the corner because I need to put in 2 more vanilla cookies than chocolate. I circled 11 vanilla cookies plus the 2 extras=13. 13-11=2. This is another way.

I solved this problem by drawing 32 cookies. Then I put my other 4 cookies in the corner because I need to put 4 less chocolate cookies than vanilla. Than I circled 16 chocolate cookies because 16+16 ekwal (equals) 32. The 16 vanilla cookies plus the 4 extras make 20 vanilla So that's how I got my answer. 20-16=4.

I used adding and subtracting for mathematics. I used cookies to act out the problem and problem solving. The clues like it has 3 less vanilla and 4 less chocolate helped me. At first I was conveused (confused) and I didn't think that I could solve the problem. But then I got the hang of it and I started liking it. I learned to fit the clue.

I'm glad you were so persistent!

page 2

From the Classroom: *Sample 2–5*

Jan. 6, 1993.

More Than, Less Than or Twice As Many?

The problem was to see how many chocolate and vanilla cookies were in a bag. I solved the problem like this. ① I had 12 thin I crosed 12 of the cookies out and put 8 of chocolate 4 of vanilla.

I took Three out of the pile and ther was 11 in chocolate and three vanilla 8+3=11

② Why did you take out three?

Did you add 3 more chocolate?

Do you mean 8 vanilla?

page 1

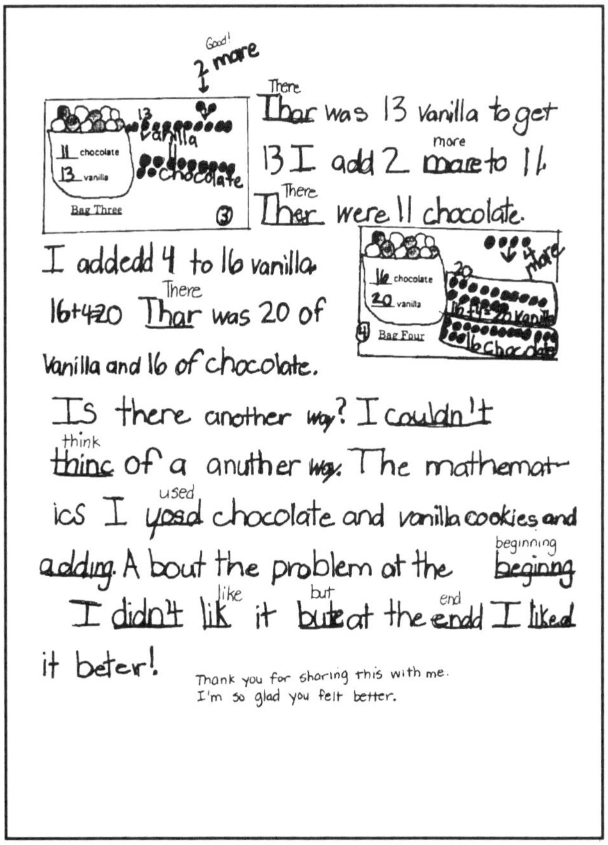
Thar was 13 vanilla to get 13 I add 2 mare to 11. Ther were 11 chocolate.

Good! 2 more

I addedd 4 to 16 vanilla 16+4=20 Thar was 20 of vanilla and 16 of chocolate.

Is there another way? I couldn't thinc of a anuther way. The mathematics I yosd chocolate and vanilla cookies and adding. A bout the problem at the beginng I didn't lik it bute at the endd I liked it beter!

Thank you for sharing this with me. I'm so glad you felt better.

page 2

In this sample, the student demonstrates that he can solve the problem accurately. However, there are some gaps in his attempt to explain the strategies he used to approach it. For example, he does not explain why he took three out of the pile of nineteen cookies in bag two or why he added 8 + 3 to get 11 cookies. He was unable to communicate another solution to each clue.

More Than, Less Than or Twice as Many?

Problem: The mother cat baked cookies and placed them into 4 bags. She put chocolate and vanilla cookies into each bag.

Then she told her baby cat that he could have all the cookies if he told her how many chocolate and vanilla cookies were in each bag. These were the four clues that the mother cat gave her baby cat to help him:

Bag One has twice as many chocolate as vanilla. Bag Two has 3 less vanilla than chocolate. Bag Three has 2 more vanilla than chocolate. Bag Four has 4 less chocolate than vanilla.

How many chocolate and vanilla cookies are in each bag?

Write your estimate:

Bag One **Bag Two** **Bag Three** **Bag Four**

Name ____________________

More Than, Less Than or Twice as Many?

Directions: show how you got your answer.

Bag One

Bag Two

Bag Three

Bag Four

Questions for Reflection

Literature Connection: *Two Ways to Count to Ten* by Ruby Dee.
King Leopard wants to find the cleaverest beast in the jungle to rule in his place someday. His plan is to find the animal who can throw a spear toward the sky and count to ten before it comes down again.

1. At the end of the year, pose the following questions:

Discussion Questions: Measurement–Length

What I Learned About Numbers

- How do you use numbers each day?
- What did you learn about numbers in second grade?
- How do you compare numbers?
- What are some things you still want to learn about numbers?
- What are some patterns that you see in the counting numbers?
- How can you change numbers?

2. Have students discuss the questions as a total group. Record their ideas on the board.
3. Tell students you are going to read another story about numbers. Ask them to listen carefully to see if there is anything more they can add to their list about numbers.
4. Read orally *Two Ways to Count to Ten.*
5. After reading the story, discuss these questions:

Questions To Ask	Possible Answers
What was the problem in the story?	• The King Leopard wanted to find the cleverest beast in the jungle.
What was the King's plan?	• He had a plan to find the cleverest beast that could throw a spear toward the sky and count to ten before it came down again.
Who was the cleverest beast and how did he solve the problem?	• The antelope solved the problem by counting to 10 by twos.
Are there other ways the antelope could have solved the problem?	• He could count by fives (5+5=10). • He could count by threes and add 1 more (3+3)+(3+1)=10.
What did you learn in the story about numbers?	• There are different ways to count to 10. • You can count to 10 by twos and fives but when you count by threes you have to add one more. It doesn't work evenly. • Counting by twos is faster.
What are some things you still want to learn about numbers?	• How to count to bigger numbers like 1,000 or 1,000,000. • How to divide 124 by 3.

6. Review *Questions for Reflection* and add new ideas to the list on the board.
7. Have students answer the questions in their journals.

★ *Encourage students to use diagrams, graphs, pictures and symbols to help answer the questions.*

8. Compare students' responses to their journal entry on *What I Already Know About Numbers.* You will gain information about:
   - whether they have expanded their knowledge of the numeration system and observed patterns.
   - their development of number sense.
   - how they use numbers in the real world.
   - whether they have increased their understanding of the concepts of whole number operations.
   - how they select and use computation to solve problems.
   - whether they have grown in their ability to express themselves in print.
   - growth in their attitude towards mathematics.
   - the effectiveness of your mathematics program.
9. Compare each students' response to *Questions for Reflection* at the beginning of the school year.

From the Classroom: *September*

I use numbers to count my crayon box. There are 144.

I want to learn 100 + 100.

In September, the student uses numbers to count the contents of a crayon box.

From the Classroom: *June*

I use numbers each day by dialing the phone to call my dad at work. by counting things out to make sure there are enough. to tell what month. date and year it is. to tell what time it is. to add and subtract and when I cook or weigh myself.

I want to learn how fast tires can go and how much liquid they put in crayons and more about algebra.

In June, her view of numbers is expanded to move beyond counting to measurement, calculation and a variety of daily life experiences such as cooking. What she wants to learn in mathematics also indicates a broader view of numbers through personal research. Her ability to communicate her ideas in print has grown.

Suggestions For Other Assessment Questions

Patterns

- What is a pattern?
- Make a pattern using pattern blocks and tell about your pattern.

Counting, Grouping and Place Value

- Count the objects and tell about the strategy you used.
- Is there another way you could have counted the objects?
- How many objects were there? How do you know?

Measurement: Weight

- What do the terms *heavy* and *light* mean?
- Name two things that are heavier or lighter than you.
- Explain how you know they are heavier or lighter than you.

What I Already Know About Addition

- How do we use addition each day?
- Why does 4 + 8 = 12?
- Write your own addition word problem for 34 + 17 and tell how you solved the problem.
- What are some other strategies you can use to solve an addition problem?

How Many Ways? *(Discrete Mathematics)*

If you have 3 shirts and 2 pairs of pants, how many days in a row can you wear a different outfit?

- How did you solve the problem?
- Is there another way you could have solved the problem?
- What patterns did you see?
- How did you feel about the problem?
- What if there were 3 shirts and 3 pairs of pants?

What I Learned Today

- What did you learn about mathematics today?
- How can this help you to become a better problem solver?

Third Grade

Questions For Reflection
What I Already Know About Mathematics

Math Exploration 1
Geometric Solids
Literature Connection: *If You Look Around You*

Math Exploration 2
Eight Dinner Elsie (Multiplication)
Literature Connection: *Six Dinner Sid*

Questions for Reflection
What I Learned About Mathematics

Suggestions For Other Assessment Questions

Questions for Reflection

1. At the beginning of the school year, pose the following questions:

Questions For Reflection
What I Already Know About Mathematics
• What did you learn in mathematics last year? (give examples)
• What were the things you found easy in mathematics last year?
• What were the things you found hard in mathematics last year?
• What do you do when you don't understand a problem?
• What are some ways that you use mathematics each day?
• What would you like to learn in mathematics this year?

2. Have students discuss the questions as a total group. Record their ideas on the board.
3. Have students answer the questions in their journals.
   ⋆ *Encourage students to use diagrams, graphs, pictures and symbols to help answer the questions.*
4. The journal entries will give you information about:
   - students' perceived strengths and weaknesses in mathematics.
   - how they define the content of mathematics.
   - their attitude towards mathematics.
   - their approach to problem-solving.
   - how they use mathematics in their daily lives.
5. Save the journal entries and use them to compare each student's response to questions for reflection at the end of the school year. (See *From the Classroom,* page 77).

Math Exploration 1: Geometric Solids

Literature Connection: *If You Look Around You* by Fulvio Testa
This story offers colorful pictures that illustrate how the reader can learn about geometry while observing things in the environment.

1. Tell students they will be studying geometric solids.
   Ask this question: *"What is a geometric solid?"*
2. Remind students to listen carefully as you read *If You Look Around You.*
   Ask them to pay close attention to the geometry in the story.
3. After reading this book, ask these questions:

Questions To Ask	Possible Answers
What were the geometric solids mentioned in the book?	• Cylinder • Cube • Cone • Sphere
What are some objects in real-life that look like each of the geometric solids?	• A baseball is a sphere. • A drum is a cylinder. • An ice cube is a cube. • A party hat can be a cone.
What is a geometric solid?	• It is a 3-D shape. • It has length, width and height.

4. During the unit on geometric solids, provide these hands on opportunities:
   - Provide time for students to freely explore three-dimensional geometric solids (cube, cylinder, sphere, rectangular solid/prism, pyramid and cone). Have them describe the characteristics of each solid and discuss their similarities and differences.
   - Play *Mystery Bag* with the students. Have one student place a geometric solid in a bag and then describe it to other students until they can correctly name the hidden object.
   - Ask students to identify objects in their classroom and in their world that look like each of the geometric solids.
   - Have students find different ways to sort and classify the geometric solids. (Shapes that roll and don't roll; shapes with flat and curved surfaces and shapes with only flat surfaces). Then, have students use Activity Sheet 3-A to create Venn diagrams and compare two geometric solids, as illustrated below:

From the Classroom: *Sample 3–1*

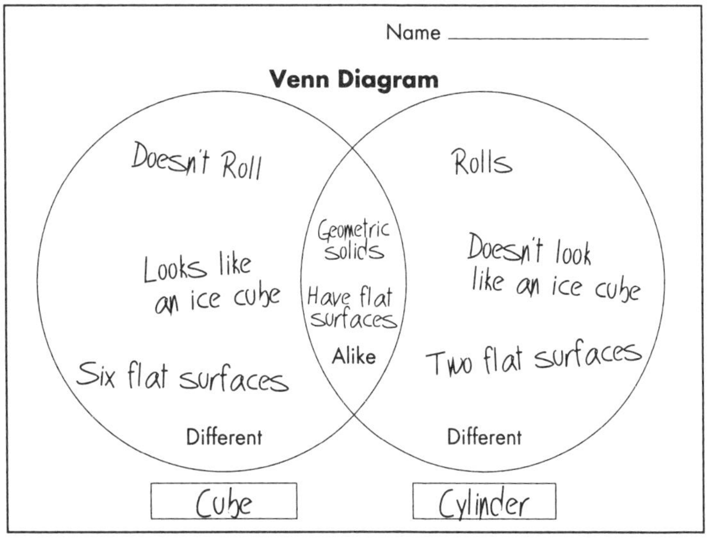

Here, the student demonstrates his ability to make comparisons and show how two geometric solids are alike and different. The task requires the student to share his ideas in an organized manner using a Venn diagram.

- Use Activity Sheets 3-B, 3-C and 3-D to have students construct geometric solids with these paper cut-outs.
- Have students construct geometric solids using clay and toothpicks. Identify faces, edges and vertices. Then, have them study the solids and complete Activity Sheet 3-E.

5. When the unit on geometric solids is complete, pose the following discussion questions about geometric solids.

Discussion Questions: Geometric Solids

- What is a geometric solid?
- Make a list of objects that look like each of the geometric solids?
- Which geometric solids roll and which geometric solids don't roll? Explain why.
- What is a face, edge and vertex?
- Describe different geometric solids using terms such as: face, edge and vertex.
- Compare two geometric solids. How are they alike and different?

6. Have students answer the questions in their journals.
   ★ *Encourage students to use diagrams, charts and pictures to help explain their answers.*
7. Use journal entries to assess students' level of understanding of geometric solids and their ability to express what they know. The following examples demonstrate a range of student responses that is likely to occur in your classroom.

From the Classroom: *Sample 3–2*

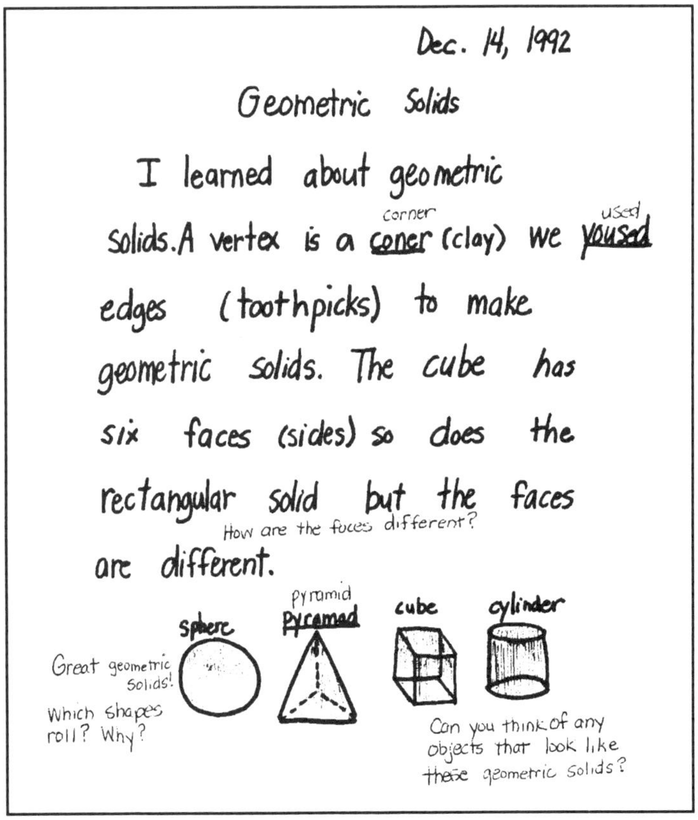
Dec. 14, 1992

Geometric Solids

I learned about geometric solids. A vertex is a coner (corner) (clay) we yousd (used) edges (toothpicks) to make geometric solids. The cube has six faces (sides) so does the rectangular solid but the faces are different. (How are the faces different?)

sphere Pycamad (pyramid) cube cylinder

Great geometric Solids!
Which shapes roll? Why?
Can you think of any objects that look like these geometric solids?

In this sample, the student demonstrates some knowledge of geometric solids but all questions are not answered and ideas need further explanation. There are no apparent misunderstandings. However, the student needs to add more detail to demonstrate full competence in expressing his knowledge.

From the Classroom: *Sample 3–3*

In this sample, the student uses appropriate mathematic vocabulary to describe geometric solids. She has organized her information in a coherent chart and has found real world examples of geometry. All discussion questions were answered.

December 14, 1992

Geometric Solids

I learned about geometric solids. The cylinder has two flat surfaces. It also has one cerved side. A flat side is called a face. (Good!) A corner is called a vertex. There are edges (What are the edges?) on a geometric solid. The cone has a point at the top. It also has one cerved serface. But it only has one flat serface. The cube is made up of little squears (squares) and points and edges. The little squears are the faces. (6 faces) It has 12 edges too. The pyramid has a point at the top too. But it is all flat faces shaped

page 1

like triangulus (triangles) and one squar. The rectangular prisum is almost like a cube. It looks like a streched cube. The sphere is all one face curved into a ball like shape. It is also very very round.

Witch Roll	Witch Don't	Why some roll and some don't.
sphere	pyramid	The ones that roll have curved faces.
cylinder	cube	But the ones that don't roll don't have curved faces.
cone	rectangular prisum	

Things that are Real: sphere – ball, balloons; cylinder – trash can, cup, soup can; cone – ice cream cone, party hat, snow cone holder; pyramid – Egiption pyramid; cube – box, pen box; rectangular prisum – box of klenex, tub, book.

You learned lots of things about geometric solids.

page 2

Name ______________________________

Venn Diagram

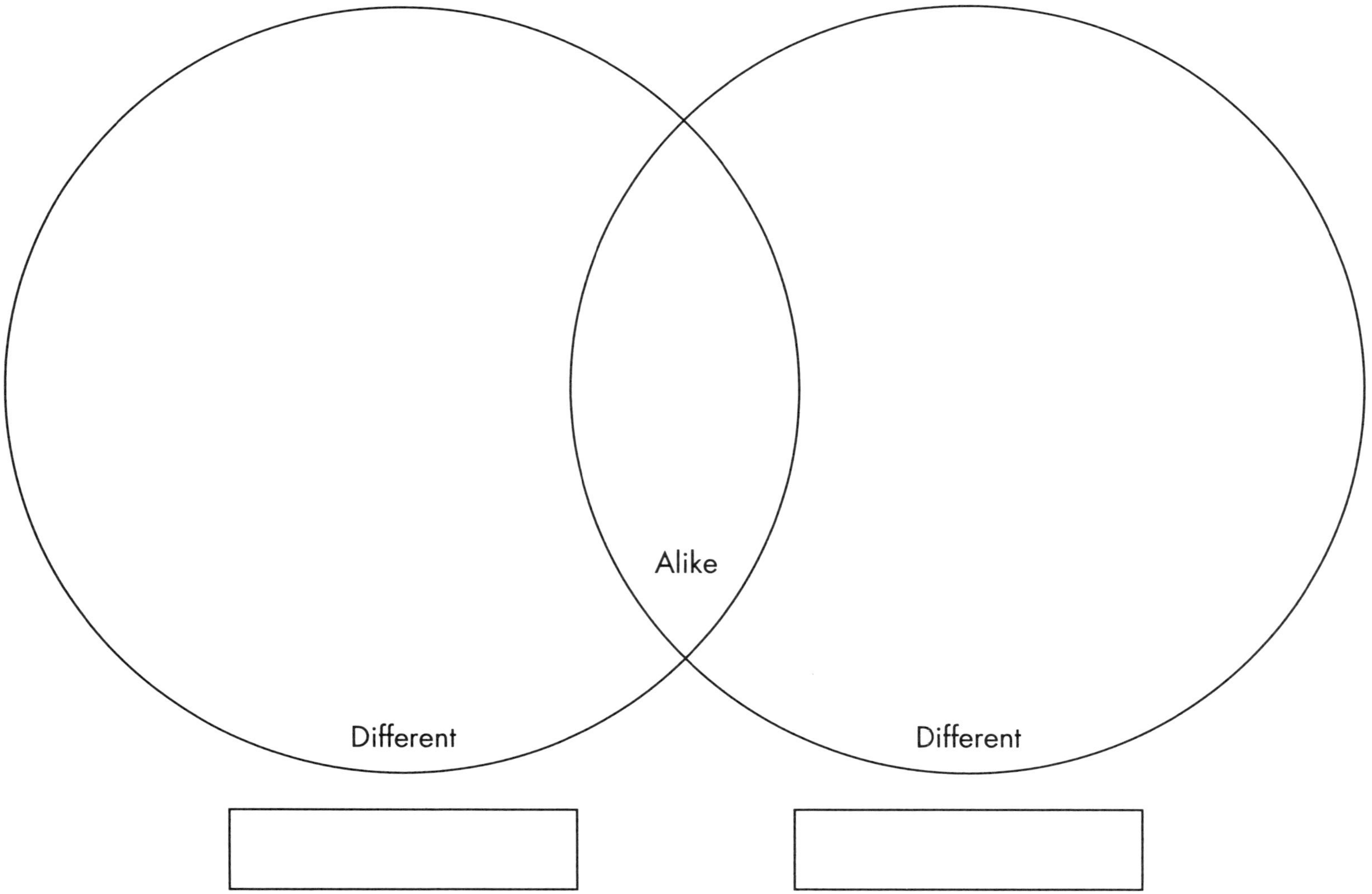

Cut out the shape.
Which geometric solid can you make by folding along the dotted lines?

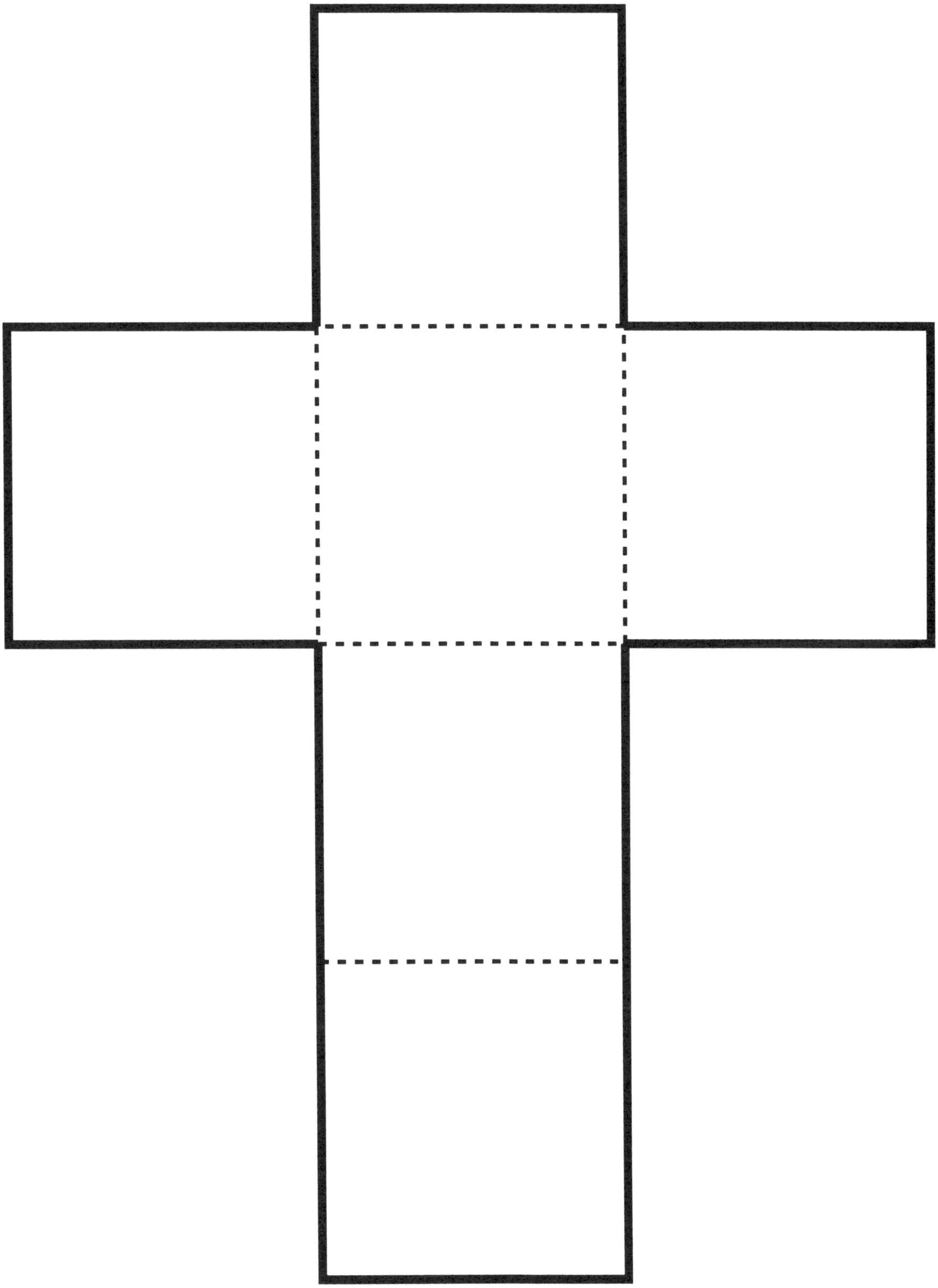

Cut out the shape.
Which geometric solid can you make by folding along the dotted lines?

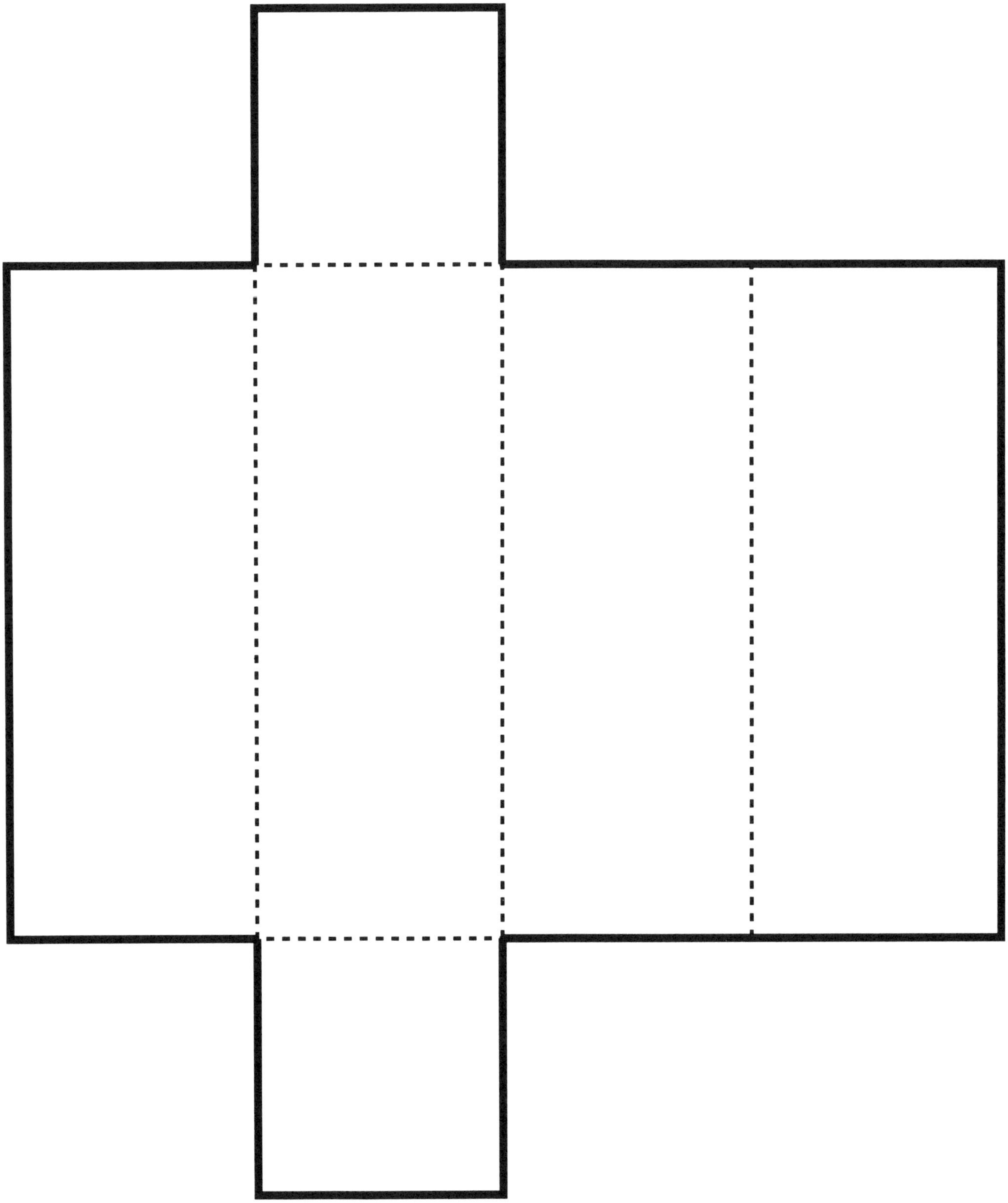

Cut out the shape.
Which geometric solid can you make by folding along the dotted lines?

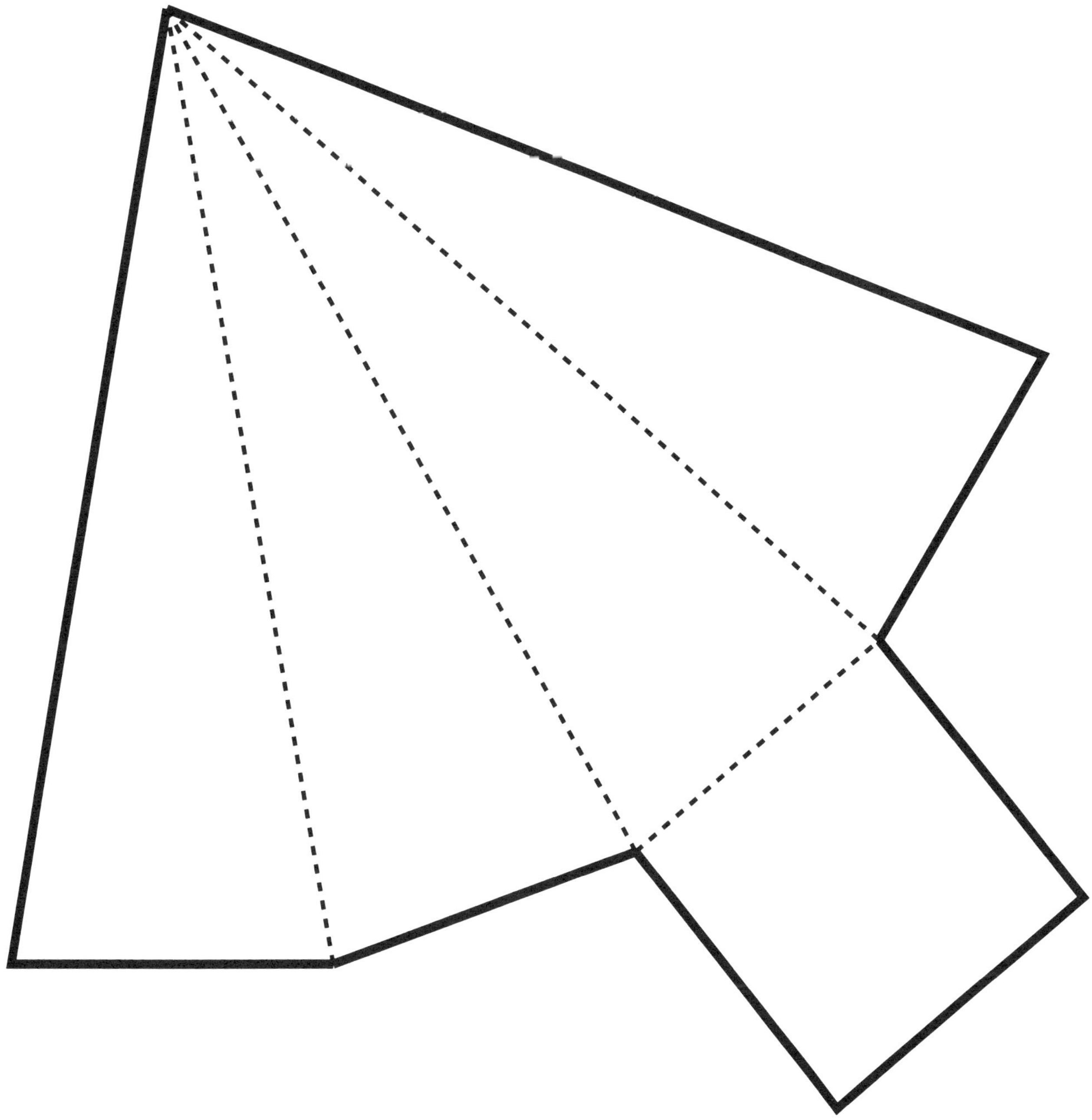

Name ____________________________

Make each geometric solid using toothpicks and clay.
Count the number of faces, edges and vertices. Record your results.

Geometric Solid	Faces	Edges	Vertices
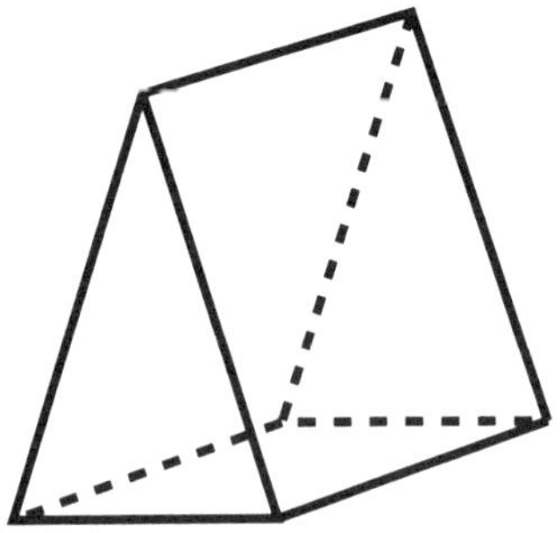			
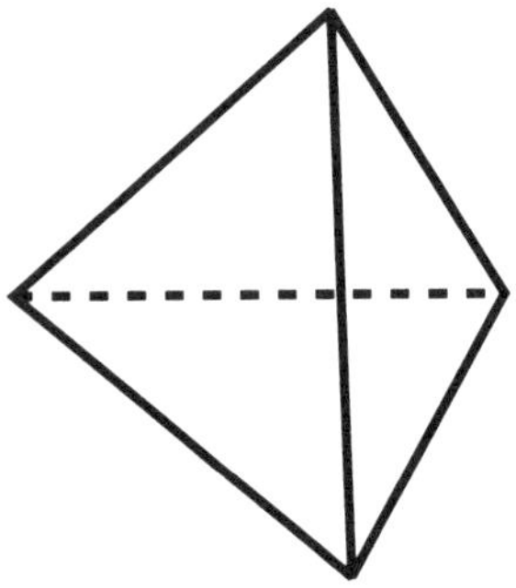			
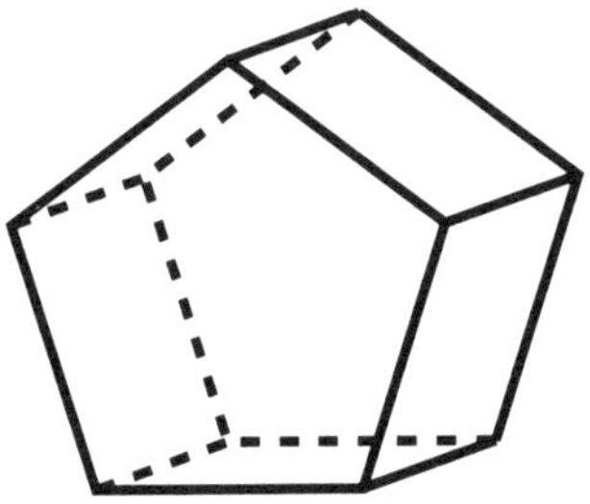			
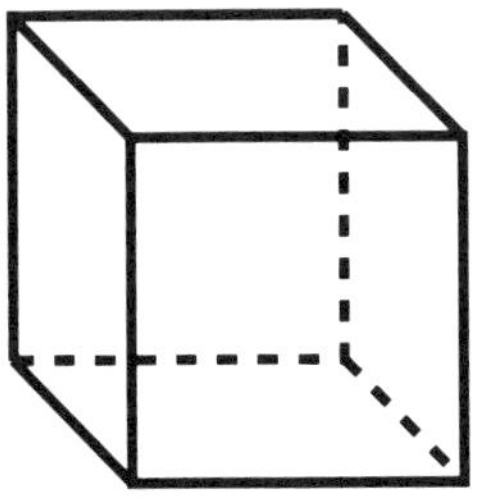			

Math Exploration 2: Eight Dinner Elsie *(Multiplication)*

Literature Connection: *Six Dinner Sid* by Inga Moore
The story of a clever cat who lives in six different houses and eats six dinners a night until his owners discover what he's been up to when he is taken to the vet six different times.

1. Read orally *Six Dinner Sid.*
2. After reading the story, ask these questions and record student responses for the group to see:

Questions To Ask	Possible Answers
How many dinners did Six Dinner Sid have in one night?	• 6
How could we find out how many dinners he had in two nights?	Students brainstorm ideas: • Add 6+6 • Multiply 2 x 6 (2 groups of 6) • Draw pictures: ❍ ❍ ❍ ❍ ❍ ❍ • Use objects ❍ ❍ ❍ ❍ ❍ ❍
How many dinners did Six Dinner Sid have in 2 nights?	• 12
How many dinners did he have in 3 nights? 4 nights? 5 nights? 6 nights? one week?	• Students continue to discuss various strategies used to answer each question. (18, 24, 30, 36, 42)
How could we find out how many dinners he had in two weeks?	Students brainstorm ideas: • 42 + 42 • 2 x 42 (2 weeks with 42 dinners in each week)
How many dinners did he have in 2 weeks?	• 84

3. Tell students that they are going to work in pairs to solve a new problem for a friend of *Six Dinner Sid.*
4. **Introduce the Problem**
   Eight Dinner Elsie lived in eight houses. She had eight different dinners each night. How many dinners did *Eight Dinner Elsie* have in one week? two weeks? three weeks? four weeks?
5. **Materials**
   - Activity Sheet 3-F (one for each student)
   - Counters (i.e., chips, cubes)
   - Calculator
   - Pencil
6. **Instructions for Students**
   - Read the problem carefully.
   - Discuss different strategies that you might use to solve the problem.
   - Choose a strategy. You can use counters and/or calculators.
   - Solve the problem and show your work.
   - Record your answers on the activity sheet.

7. Have students share their solutions to the problem and the strategies that they used.
8. Discuss the following questions with the class:

Discussion Questions: Eight Dinner Elsie

- Describe the problem in your own words.
- How did you solve the problem? What strategies did you use?
- Is there another way you could have solved the problem?
- How many dinners did Eight Dinner Elsie have?
- What mathematics did you learn through this activity?
- How did you feel about the problem? Why?

9. Have students answer the questions in their journals.
   ★ *Encourage students to use diagrams, charts, pictures and symbols to help explain their answers.*
10. Use journal entries to assess students' ability to select an appropriate problem-solving strategy and describe it coherently. Students must be able to apply mathematical concepts to solve the problem. The emphasis here is more on the child's ability to communicate the process than on the correct answer.
11. **Answer Key**
    - In one week, she had 56 dinners.
    - In two weeks, she had 112 dinners.
    - In three weeks, she had 168 dinners.
    - In four weeks, she had 224 dinners.

From the Classroom: *Sample 3–4*

In this sample, the student uses repeated addition and multiplication to arrive at an accurate total on her activity sheet. Her journal entry indicates an organized and coherent approach to the problem, a clear description of sophisticated strategies and a thorough discussion of the questions.

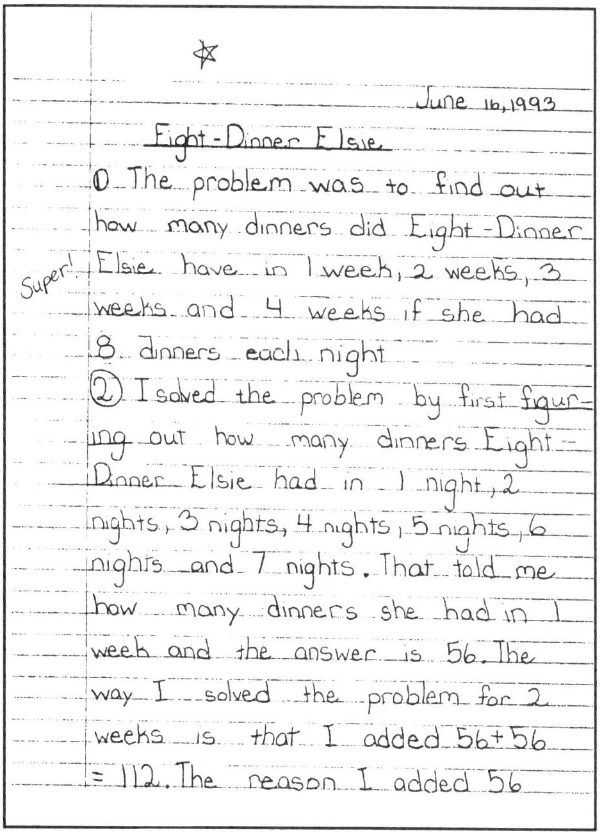

☆

June 16, 1993

Eight-Dinner Elsie

① The problem was to find out how many dinners did Eight-Dinner Elsie have in 1 week, 2 weeks, 3 weeks and 4 weeks if she had 8 dinners each night

Super!

② I solved the problem by first figuring out how many dinners Eight-Dinner Elsie had in 1 night, 2 nights, 3 nights, 4 nights, 5 nights, 6 nights and 7 nights. That told me how many dinners she had in 1 week and the answer is 56. The way I solved the problem for 2 weeks is that I added 56+56 = 112. The reason I added 56

page 1

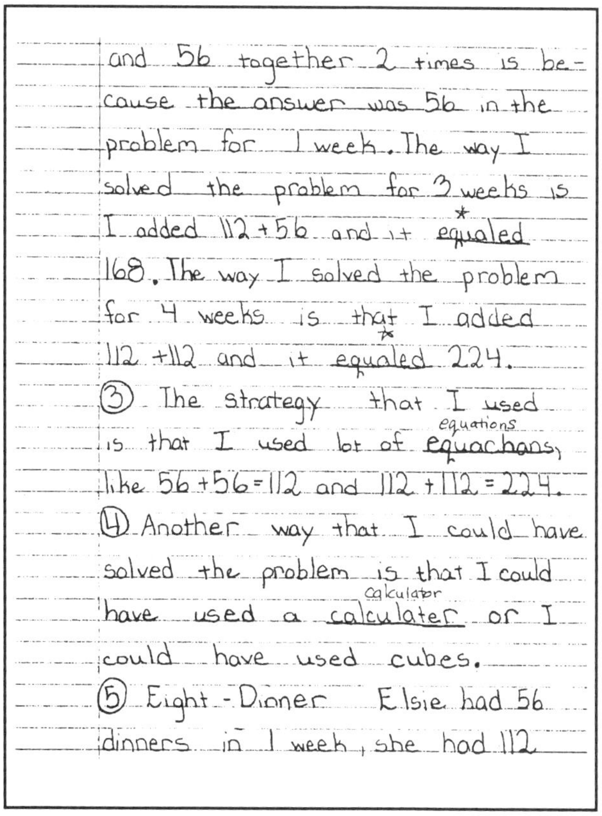

and 56 together 2 times is because the answer was 56 in the problem for 1 week. The way I solved the problem for 3 weeks is I added 112+56 and it equaled* 168. The way I solved the problem for 4 weeks is that I added 112+112 and it equaled* 224.

③ The strategy that I used is that I used lot of equachans [equations], like 56+56=112 and 112+112=224.

④ Another way that I could have solved the problem is that I could have used a calculater [calculator] or I could have used cubes.

⑤ Eight-Dinner Elsie had 56 dinners in 1 week, she had 112

page 2

Sample 3–4: *continued*

dinners in 2 weeks, she had 168 dinners in 3 weeks and she had 224 dinners in 4 weeks.

(6) The mathematics that I learned more about is more multiplacation and a lot more adding because I did a lot of equachans [equations].

(7) I felt good about the problem because it was hard and it teaches you a lot of math because if you keep on doing a lot of equachans [equations] like I did, then you keep on getting better and better at math.

Nice job!
I enjoyed reading this!!
How did you decide on the equations to use?

Wonderful!

page 3

Eight-Dinner Elsie

Wonderful! ★

PROBLEM: Eight-Dinner Elsie lived in eight houses. She had eight different dinners each night. How many dinners did Eight-Dinner Elsie have in one week? two weeks? three weeks? four weeks?

Show your work:

one week 16+16+16+8=56 7×8=56	two weeks 56 + 56 = 112 2×56=112	three weeks 3×56=168 112 + 56 = 168 56 + 56 + 56 = 168	four weeks 112 + 112 = 224 112×2=224
one night 8	two nights 8+8=16	three nights 8+8+8=24 3×8=24	four nights 4×8=32 8+8+8+8=32 16+16=32
five nights 5×8=40 8+8+8+8+8=40 16+16+8=40	six nights 6×8=48 16+16+16=48	seven nights 7×8=56 16+16+16+8=56	

Answers: In one week, she had 56 dinners.

In two weeks, she had 112 dinners.

In three weeks, she had 168 dinners.

In four weeks, she had 224 dinners.

Write about how you got your answers.

page 4

From the Classroom: *Sample 3–5*

In this sample, the student demonstrates that he can solve the problem accurately. However, there are some gaps in his attempt to explain the problem and the strategies he used to approach it. He clearly explains how he got his answer for the number of dinners Eight Dinner Elsie had in one week but does not discuss how he used division, addition and multiplication to solve the rest of the problem.

June. 16, '99

Eight-Dinner Elsie

What was the problen? The problem was to find out howmany dinners elsie eat in one day and one week two weeks three weeks four weeks makes 224.

(Don't we already know that she eats 8 dinners each day?)

2. How did you solve the problem? I solved the problem by using a calculatar.

3. What strategies did you use. I used divistion adding and multapulcation

Is there another way you could have solved the problem? I don't thik so

What about using objects?

page 1

5 Howmany dinners did elsie have? 56 because 7X8=56 the 7 means 7 nights the 8 means how many dinners she got in one night and thats how I got 56.

here is the Calculater

I pushed the 7 and the X sein and then the 8 and it equaled 56.

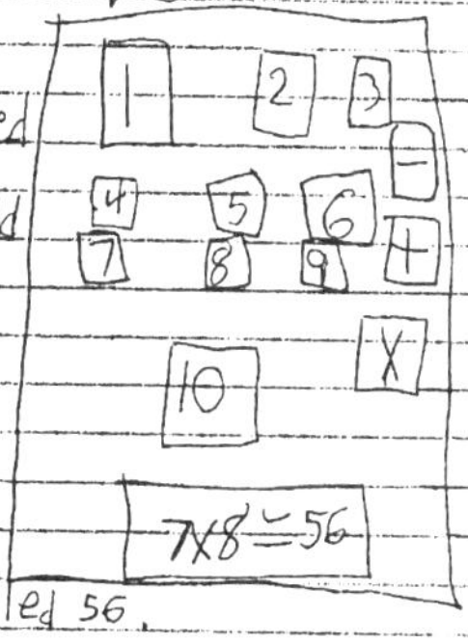

6 What mathematics did you learn? I learned the divistion is like multapulcation.

7. I felt hungry when I did the problem.

page 2

Name ______________________________

Eight Dinner Elsie

Problem: Eight Dinner Elsie lived in eight houses. She had eight different dinners each night. How many dinners did Eight Dinner Elsie have in one week? two weeks? three weeks? four weeks?

Show your work:

Answer: In one week, she had ________ dinners.

In two weeks, she had ________ dinners.

In three weeks, she had ________ dinners.

In four weeks, she had ________ dinners.

Write about how you got your answers.

Questions for Reflection

1. At the end of the school year, pose the following questions:

Questions For Reflection

What I Learned About Mathematics

- Did you like math this year? Why?
- What did you learn in mathematics this year? (give examples)
- What do you still need to work on in mathematics?
- What math activities did you like best?
- What do you do when you don't understand a problem?
- What are some ways that you use mathematics each day?
- What would you like to learn in mathematics next year?

2. Have students discuss the questions as a total group. Record their ideas on the board.
3. Have students answer the questions in their journals.
   ★ *Encourage students to use diagrams, graphs, pictures and symbols to help explain their answers.*
4. Compare students' responses to their journal entry on *What I Already Know About Mathematics.* You will gain information about:
   - changes in students' perceived strengths and weakness in mathematics.
   - whether they have expanded their view about the content of mathematics.
   - growth in their attitude towards mathematics.
   - whether they have learned new approaches to problem-solving.
   - how they use mathematics in their daily lives.
   - whether they have grown in their ability to express themselves in print.
   - the effectiveness of your mathematics program.
5. Compare each student's response to questions for reflection at the beginning of the school year.

From the Classroom

In September, the student sees mathematics as addition, subtraction and division.

In June, his view of mathematics is expanded to move beyond the number strand to include measurement, data collecting and real-life experiences such as the architect who is designing a house. He learns to be more persistent as he develops a variety of strategies, and builds confidence in his ability to solve problems and express his ideas.

Math is counting and adding. Math helps me learn about numbers and odd and even. Math is millions of things. like adding and subtracting and division.

When I don't know the answer to a problem. I cry.

September

If you're an architect. you use math to measure the size and perimeter of houses and buildings. Math is making graphs and writing problems.

When I can't figure something out. I think about it more. and try all the strategies I know. And if that doesn't work. I go on and come back to it.

June

Suggestions For Other Assessment Questions

All About 24
- How many different ways can you tell about the number 24? (list at least 10 ways)

Addition
- Write a word problem for 243 + 165 and solve the problem.
- Write about how you solved the problem.
- Is there another way you could have solved the problem?
- What strategies do you use to solve addition problems?

What I Learned About Money
- Why do people need money?
- How much is a lot of money?
- What do you know about pennies, nickels, dimes and quarters?
- If you gave the man $1.00 for a hot dog that costs 78¢, how much change should he give you back? Tell how you got your answer.
- How many different ways can you represent $1.00?

Mental Math Strategies
- How does knowing 3 x 3 help you with 3 x 30?
- What else does knowing 3 x 3 help you with?

What I Learned About Division
- Write a definition for division.
- How do you use division in real-life?
- Write your own division word problem for 16 ÷ 3 and solve the problem.
- What is a remainder?
- What strategies do you use to solve division problems?
- How can multiplication help you solve division problems?

Calendar
- Make a calendar for this month. What patterns do you see in your calendar?
- What is the date three days after the second Tuesday this month? Tell how you got your answer.
- You have a special party 2 weeks and 4 days after the first Wednesday this month. What day will it be? Tell how you got your answer.
- Write your own calendar problem and tell how you got your answer.

Fourth Grade

Questions For Reflection
What I Already Know About Mathematics

Math Exploration 1
Multiplication
Literature Connection: *Sea Squares*

Math Exploration 2
How many Rabbits? (Patterns)
Literature Connection: *The April Rabbits*

Questions for Reflection
What I Learned About Mathematics

Suggestions For Other Assessment Questions

Questions for Reflection

1. At the beginning of the school year, pose the following questions:

> **Questions For Reflection**
>
> **What I Already Know About Mathematics**
> - What is mathematics?
> - What did you learn in mathematics last year? (give examples)
> - Did you like math last year? Why?
> - How do you use mathematics each day?
> - Are you a good problem solver? Why?
> - What do you want to learn in mathematics in fourth grade?

2. Have students discuss the questions as a total group.
   Record their ideas on the board.
3. Have students answer the questions in their journals.
   ★ *Encourage students to use diagrams, graphs, pictures and symbols to help answer the questions.*
4. The journal entries will give you information about:
   - students perceived strengths and weakness in mathematics.
   - how they define the content of mathematics.
   - their attitude towards mathematics.
   - their approach to problem-solving.
   - how they use mathematics in their daily lives.
5. Save the journal entries and use them to compare each student's response to *Questions for Reflection* at the end of the school year. (See *From the Classroom*, page 93).

Math Exploration 1: Multiplication

Literature Connection: *Sea Squares* by Joy N. Hulme
This counting book has rhymes and colorful illustrations. As students count creatures in the ocean, they learn how to square numbers.

1. Tell students they will be studying multiplication. Ask these questions:
   - What is multiplication?
   - How do we use multiplication in our daily lives?
2. Read orally *Sea Squares.* Discuss how multiplication is used in the story.
   Ask students to explain why they think the story is called *Sea Squares.*
   Have them use tiles to experiment with the square numbers represented in the book and look for patterns:

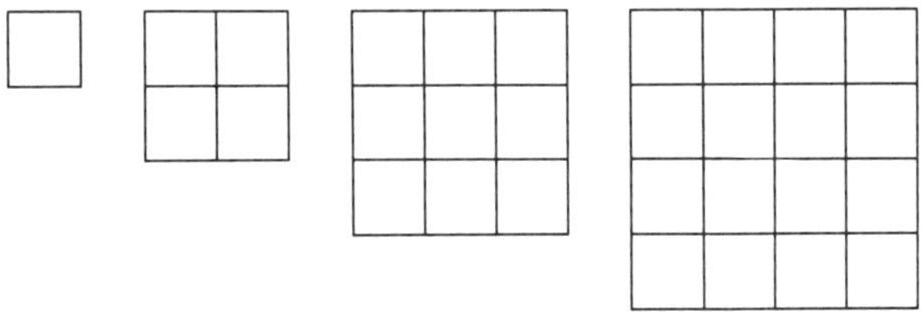

1 x 1	1
2 x 2	4
3 x 3	9
4 x 4	16

3. During the unit on multiplication, provide these hands-on opportunities:
   - Make different rectangular arrays using tiles to represent the counting numbers. Look for other patterns and make an organized list. For example:

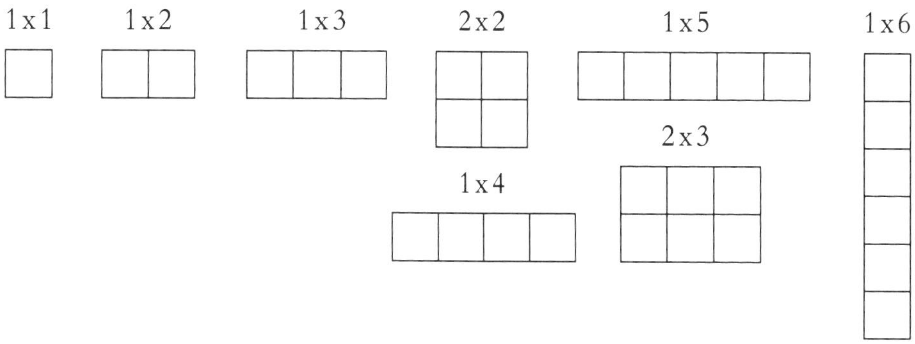

   - Have students work in groups to design a floor plan for a house and find the total area. Students will need Activity Sheet 4-A, construction paper (12″ by 18″), scissors and glue.
     a. Design each room using tiles.
     b. Cut out a representation of each room using grid paper.
     c. Label the area of each room.
     d. Glue the representations on construction paper to show the floor plan of the house.
     e. Find the total area of the house.

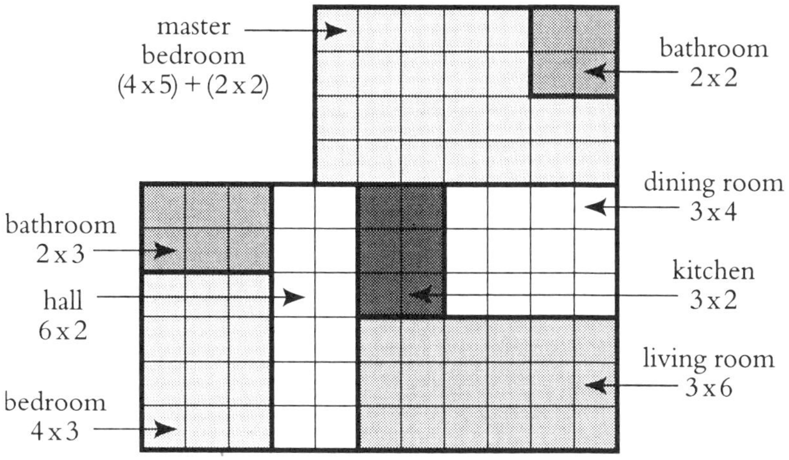

Room	Square Units
living room	18
dining room	12
kitchen	6
hall	12
bedroom	12
bathroom	6
master bedroom	24
bathroom	4
Total Area	94

From the Classroom: *Sample 4–1*

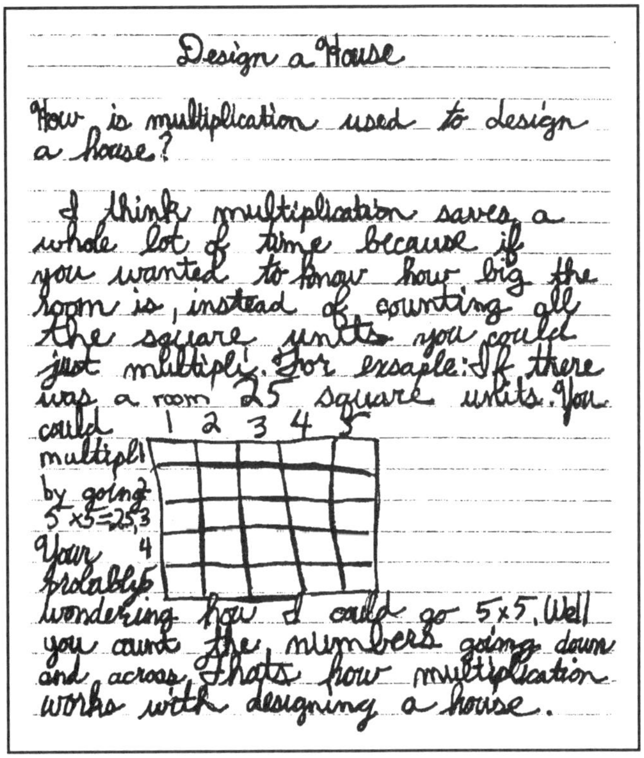
Design a House

How is multiplication used to design a house?

I think multiplication saves a whole lot of time because if you wanted to know how big the room is, instead of counting all the square units you could just multipli. For exsaple: If there was a room 25 square units. You could multipli by going 5 x5=25 Your probably wondering how I could go 5x5. Well you count the numbers going down and across. Thats how multiplication works with designing a house.

Here, the student demonstrates her intuitive understanding and application to the method used to calculate the area of a rectangle. The task requires the student to express her ideas, justify her thinking and communicate how multiplication can be used in our daily lives.

- Students write their own multiplication word problems.

From the Classroom: *Sample 4–2*

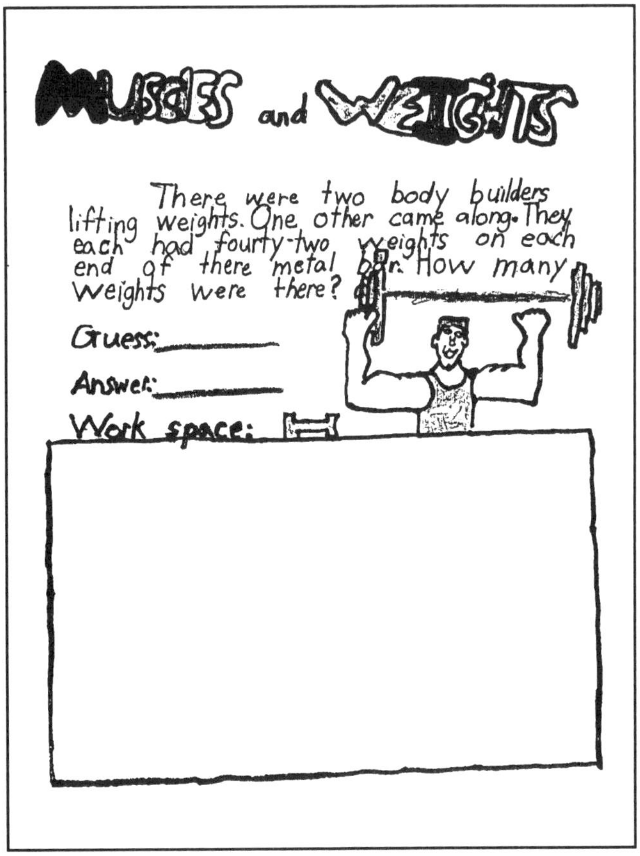
MUSCLES and WEIGHTS

There were two body builders lifting weights. One other came along. They each had fourty-two weights on each end of there metal bar. How many weights were there?

Guess:

Answer:

Work space:

Here, the student demonstrates his ability to create a word problem that utilizes multiplication concepts. The task requires the student to synthesize what he knows about multiplication, rather than respond to a computational problem created by someone else.

- Students experiment with the calculator to multiply using zeros and look for patterns:

  2 x 4 = 8
  2 x 40 = 80
  2 x 400 = 800
- Students find different ways to solve 3 x 48 and share their strategies:

$$\begin{array}{r} {}^{2}\\ 48 \\ 48 \\ \underline{48} \\ 144 \end{array}$$

$$\begin{array}{r} {}^{2}\\ 48 \\ \underline{\times 3} \\ 144 \end{array}$$

$$\begin{array}{r} 40 \\ \underline{\times 3} \\ 120 \end{array} + \begin{array}{r} 8 \\ \underline{\times 3} \\ 24 \end{array} = 144$$

4. When the unit on multiplication is complete, pose the following discussion questions about multiplication.

Discussion Questions: Multiplication

- What is multiplication?
- How do we use multiplication in our daily lives?
- How does multiplication help you to understand square numbers?
- How does knowing 3 x 5 help with 3 x 50?
- Write a word problem for 3 x 84.
  Explain how you would solve the problem.
- How can multiplication help you with division?
- How has multiplication helped you to become a better problem solver?

5. Have students answer the questions in their journals.
   ★ *Encourage students to use diagrams, graphs, pictures and symbols to explain their answers.*
6. Use journal entries to assess students' level of understanding of multiplication and their ability to express what they know. The following examples demonstrate a range of student responses that is likely to occur in your classroom.

From the Classroom: *Sample 4–3*

March 22, 1993

equal groups

Multiplication is a very important concept. It is a faster way of adding. Here are the two ways you can write it:

$$\begin{array}{r} 9 \\ \times 8 \\ \hline 72 \end{array} \qquad 9 \times 8 = 72$$

9 groups of 8

If you had 3 cans of cat food at $2.50 each, Instead of going

$$\begin{array}{r} 2.50 \\ + 2.50 \\ 2.50 \end{array}$$

you can go like this →

$$\begin{array}{r} \$2.50 \\ \times 3 \\ \hline \$7.50 \end{array}$$

Doesn't that take a lot less time? Multiplication is extremely simple to learn. All it does is take a lot of time and pradice. Multiplication is basicly the same as adding equal groups. We use multiplication in our daily live when we go to a grocery store like this:

page 1

4 TV diners cost $5.00 each. If I want to get 4 how much will it cost? MULTIPLY

$$\begin{array}{r} \$5.00 \\ \times 4 \\ \hline \$20.00 \end{array} \qquad \begin{array}{r} 5 \\ 5 \\ 5 \\ 5 \\ \hline 20 \end{array}$$

Here's another way:

I have 2 cats they hav two tags on their collar. How many tags in all? Multiply!

2x2=4

Now you got the point that multiplication is everywhere. Multiplication helps you with ~~multip~~ square numbers like this

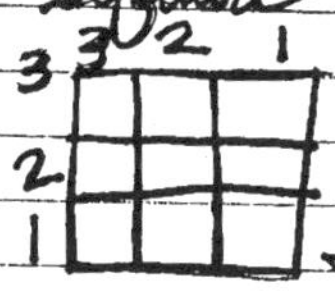

3 by 3
I makes a square

page 2

In this sample, the student uses appropriate mathematics vocabulary to describe multiplication. His journal entry indicates a thorough understanding of multiplication. All questions are answered and mathematical ideas are communicated effectively.

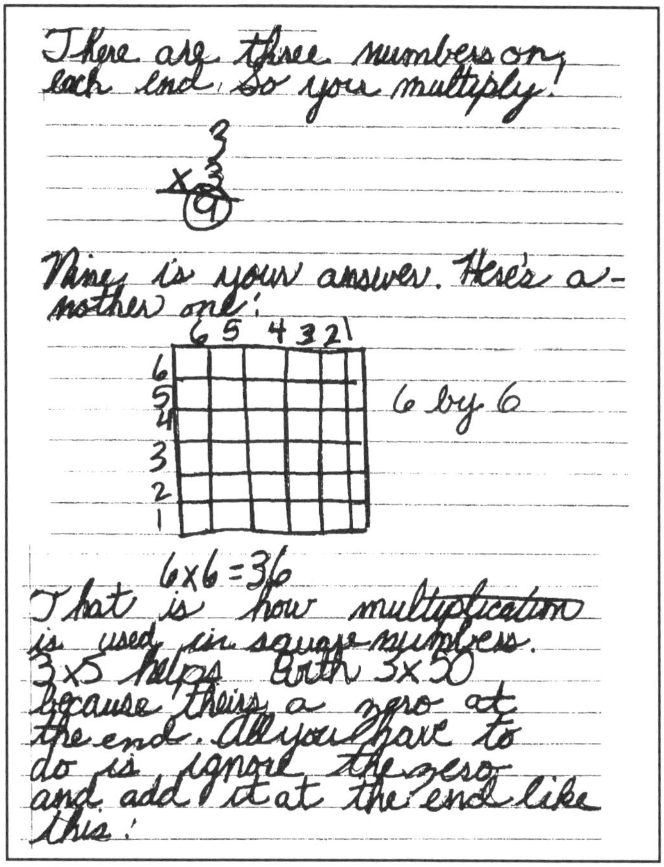

There are three numbers on each end. So you multiply!

$$\begin{array}{r} 3 \\ \times 3 \\ \hline 9 \end{array}$$

Nine is your answer. Here's a-nother one:

6 5 4 3 2 1

6 by 6

$6 \times 6 = 36$

That is how multiplication is used in square numbers.
3x5 helps with 3x50 because theirs a zero at the end. All you have to do is ignore the zero and add it at the end like this:

page 3

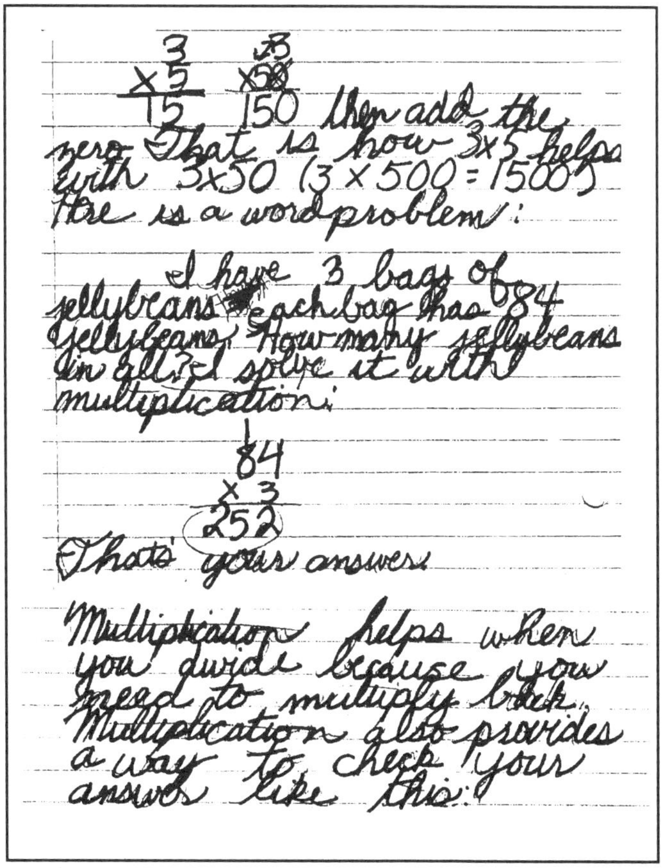

$$\begin{array}{r} 3 \\ \times 5 \\ \hline 15 \end{array} \qquad \begin{array}{r} 3 \\ \times 50 \\ \hline 150 \end{array}$$

then add the zero. That is how 3x5 helps with 3x50 (3 x 500 = 1500)
Here is a word problem:

I have 3 bags of jellybeans each bag has 84 jellybeans. How many jellybeans in all? I solve it with multiplication:

$$\begin{array}{r} 84 \\ \times 3 \\ \hline 252 \end{array}$$

That's your answer.

Multiplication helps when you divide because you need to mutiply back. Multiplication also provides a way to check your answer like this:

page 4

Sample 4–3: *continued*

6)75 six goes into
7 one time (1x 6=6) that's
where you multiply. Also
when you get into

12R3
6)75 Six goes
-6↓ into 15, 2 times
15
(2x6=12) 12 The answer
3 is 12 R 3. 12
×6
72
+3
75

you can check your answer

That is how you do it.
Multiplication has helped
me to be a better problem
solver because it is faster.
It helpes you to
speed up adding. It's
easier when you have
24 10's you can just
multiply than add.

Now you can see that
multiplication helps you
everywhere! Isn't multiplication
wonderful?!!

page 5

From the Classroom: *Sample 4–4*

March 22, 1993

① Multiplication is
where you combine
numbers. It's like
a higher level of
addition. The
multiplication sign
looks like this: x.
For example: 5×3=15.
Just do this in
your mind 5+5+5=15

② I use multiplication
daily like, the 49 ers
scored seven touch-
downs including all
the bonus points.
So I would do 7×7=49
so the 49ers scored
49 points.

③ Square numbers
are where you multiply
something by the
same number like
9×9=81.

page 1

In this sample, the student demonstrates an understanding of multiplication. There are no apparent misunderstandings. However, the student needs to add more detail to demonstrate full competence in expressing her knowledge. For example, she does not clearly state the relationship between multiplication and division.

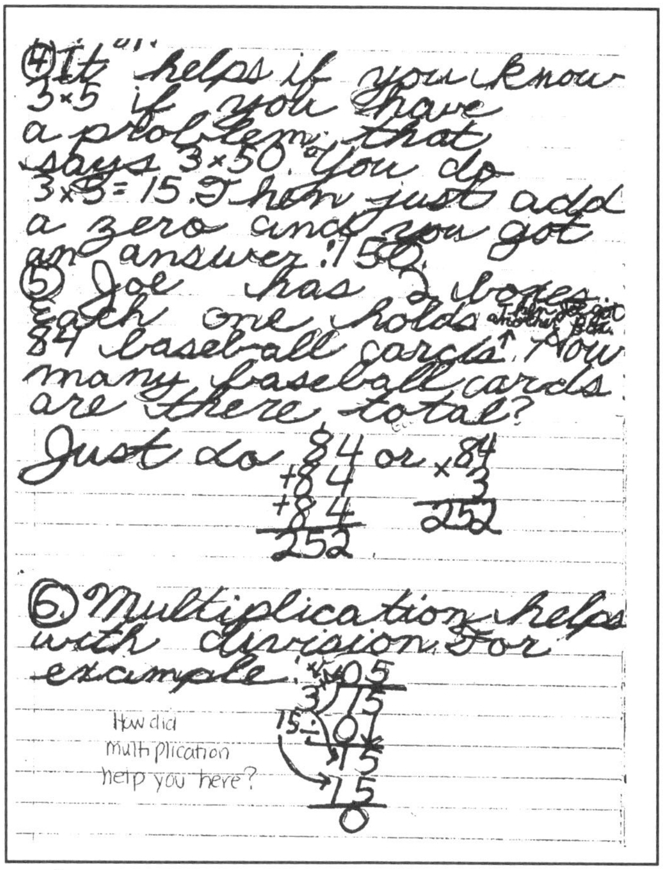

4) It helps if you know 3×5 if you have a problem that says 3×50. You do 3×5 = 15. Then just add a zero and you got an answer: 150.

5) Joe has 3 boxes. Each one holds 84 baseball cards. How many baseball cards are there total?

Just do 84 + 84 + 84 = 252 or 84 × 3 = 252

6) Multiplication helps with division. For example: 3)75 = 05, 0, 75, 75, 0

How did multiplication help you here?

page 2

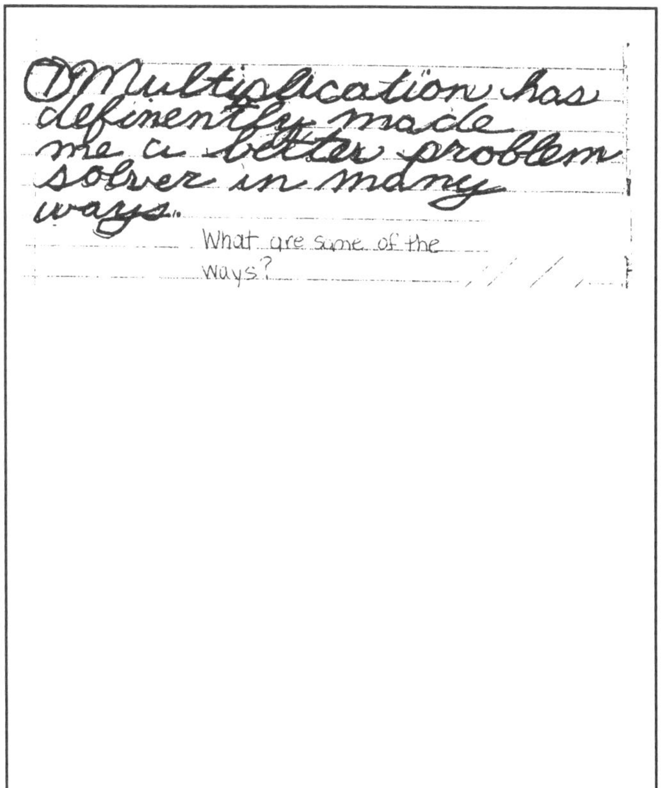

7) Multiplication has definently made me a better problem solver in many ways.

What are some of the ways?

page 3

Name ____________________

Math Exploration 2: How Many Rabbits?

Literature Connection: *The April Rabbits* by David Cleveland
The story begins on the first of April with one rabbit. Each day of the month, the number of rabbits increases by the amount represented by the day's date.

1. **Introduce the Problem**
   How many rabbits will there be at the end of the month if one rabbit appears on the first day of April, two rabbits appear on the second day of April, three rabbits appear on the third day of April and so on?
2. Students discuss the problem as a total group to make sure they understand the problem.
3. Students can work in pairs to make an estimate for how many rabbits there will be at the end of the month. Have students write in their journals to explain why they chose their estimates. Record all estimates on a class chart.
   ★ *It is important to let students know they will have opportunities to revise their estimates as they gather data during the month.*
4. **Materials**
   - Activity Sheet 4-B (55 sheets)
   - Scissors
   - Glue
   - Crayons or colored pencils
   - Butcher paper to display the rabbits each day
5. **Instructions for Students** *(The exploration will take an entire month)*
   - Read a page from the book each day of the month and add the appropriate number of rabbits to the chart. A different pair of students can be responsible for decorating the rabbits and displaying the rabbits each day in an organized manner.
     ★ *The class can decide as a total group how to organize the rabbits.*
   - Discuss any patterns that occur.
   - Work in pairs, from time to time during the month, to revise your estimates and justify your reasoning. Eliminate any estimates on the class chart that are not reasonable.
6. At the end of the month, students evaluate their results in a class discussion. They can share various strategies for solving the problems.

Some strategies that can be used to solve the problem:

Recursive Sequence

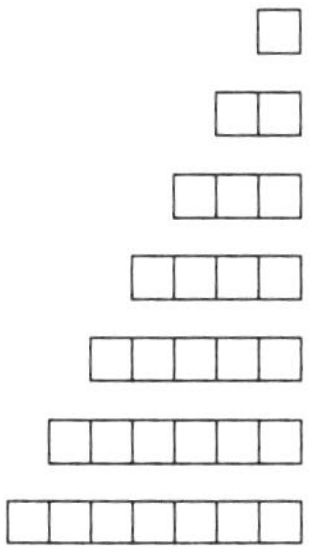

1 = 1
1 + 2 = 3
1 + 2 + 3 = 6
1 + 2 + 3 + 4 = 10
1 + 2 + 3 + 4 + 5 = 15
1 + 2 + 3 + 4 + 5 + 6 = 21
1 + 2 + 3 + 4 + 5 + 6 + 7 = 28

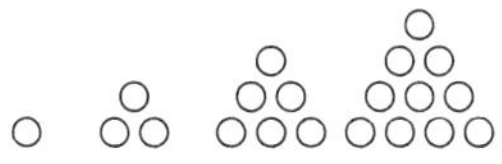

These are the triangular numbers.

Make with blue tiles:

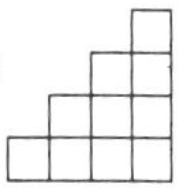

Partner copies with red tiles:

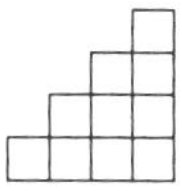

Form a rectangle and describe.
How much is half of the rectangle?

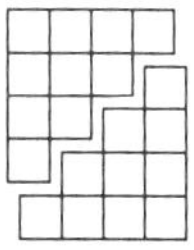

- 4 by 5 = 20 tiles
- $\frac{4 \times 5}{2} = \frac{20}{2} = 10$ tiles

Formula for the sum of the first whole integers: $\frac{(n)(n + 1)}{2}$

How many rabbits in April?★

Rabbits: $\frac{(29)(30)}{2} = \frac{870}{2} = 435$

★As there are no rabbits in the book on April 30, the answer is 435.

7. Discuss the following questions with the class:

Discussion Questions: How Many Rabbits?

- Describe the problem in your own words.
- What was your estimate?
- How did you choose your estimate?
- Did you change your estimate? Why?
- How many rabbits were there at the end of April?
- Is there another way you could have solved the problem?
- What mathematics did you use?

8. Have students answer the questions in their journals.
   ⋆ *Encourage students to use diagrams, charts, pictures and symbols to help explain their answers.*
9. Use journal entries to assess students' ability to select an appropriate problem-solving strategy and describe it coherently. Students must be able to apply mathematical concepts to solve the problem. The emphasis here is more on the child's ability to communicate the process than on the correct answer.

From the Classroom: *Sample 4–5*

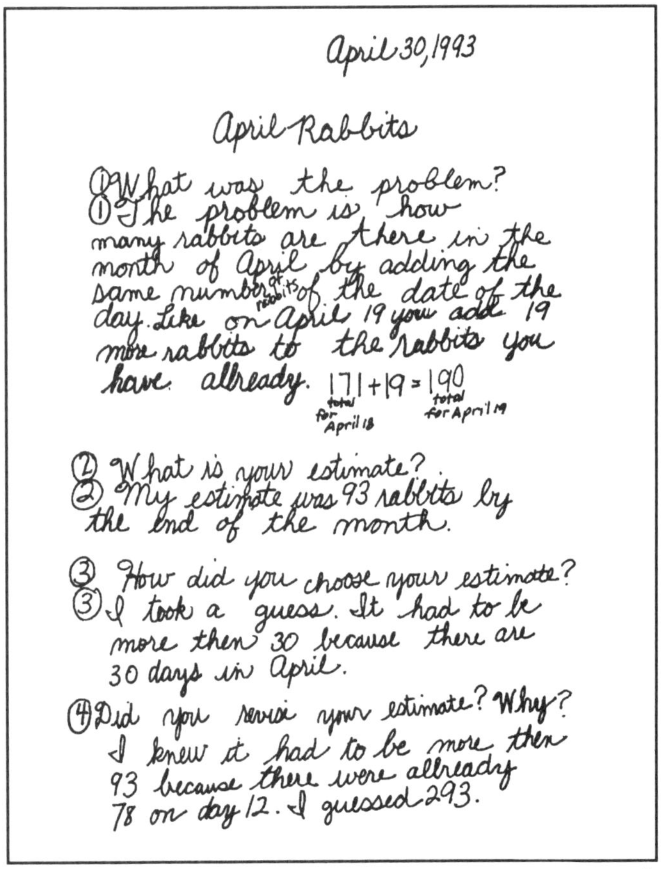
April 30, 1993

April Rabbits

① What was the problem?
① The problem is how many rabbits are there in the month of April by adding the same number of rabbits of the date of the day. Like on April 19 you add 19 more rabbits to the rabbits you have allready. 171 + 19 = 190
total for April 18 total for April 19

② What is your estimate?
② My estimate was 93 rabbits by the end of the month.

③ How did you choose your estimate?
③ I took a guess. It had to be more then 30 because there are 30 days in April.

④ Did you revise your estimate? Why?
I knew it had to be more then 93 because there were allready 78 on day 12. I guessed 293.

page1

In this sample, the student demonstrates an understanding of the problem. He is able to explain his strategy and describe another way to solve the problem using a pattern he has identified. He learns to justify his estimation based on information gathered.

(4) How many rabbits were there.

(4) There were 435 because there were no rabbits on April 30. Then there wold be

$$\begin{array}{r} 435 \\ +\ 30 \\ \hline 465 \end{array}$$

(5) How did you solve the problem?

(5) 1+2+3+4+5+6+7+8+9+10+11+12+13+14+15+16+17+18+19+20+21+22+23+24 25+26+27+28+29=435

I used a calculator.

(6) Another way-

(6) 1+2=3 3+3=6 6+4=10 10+5=15

15+6=21 21+7=28 28+8=36 and so on.

(7) What mathematics did you learn?

(7) I learned there was a pattern.

1 > 2
3 > 3
6 > 4
10 > 5
15 and so on

You didn't have to go 1+2+3+4+5+6+7=28 you ~~go~~ add to what you have allready. 21+7=28

I also learned you can make another estimate when you get more information. There were alot more rabbits then I thought.

page2

From the Classroom: *Sample 4–6*

In this sample, the student demonstrates that she can solve the problem. However, there are some gaps in her attempt to explain the problem and the strategies she used to approach it. When defining the problem, she does not explain that the number of rabbits appearing each day should match the date. This information would have been helpful in her attempt to explain the strategy she used.

April 30, 1993

April Rabbits

The problem was how many rabbits are there in April. My estimate was 125 and then I made it 200 because each day the number got much bicer.

There were 435 rabbits at the end of April. I added a nother number each day.

I learned to add the number each day 1+2+3-4+5+6+7+8+9+10+11+12+13+14+15+16+17+18+19+20+21+22+23+24+25+26+27+28+29+

It was fun to see all the rabbits.

page 1

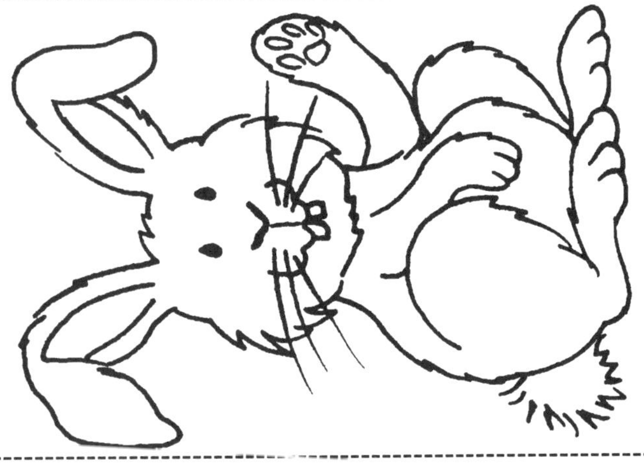

Questions for Reflection: What I Learned About Mathematics

1. At the end of the school year, pose the following questions:

Questions For Reflection
What I Learned About Mathematics
• What is mathematics?
• Did you like math this year? Why?
• What did you learn in mathematics this year? (Give examples)
• What do you still need to work on in mathematics?
• What math activities did you like best?
• How do you use mathematics in your daily life?
• What would you like to learn next year in mathematics?

2. Have students discuss the questions as a total group. Record their ideas on the board.
3. Have students write in their journals.
   ★ *Encourage students to use diagrams, graphs, pictures and symbols to help answer the questions.*
4. Compare students' responses to their journal entry on *What I Already Know About Mathematics.* You will gain information about:
   - changes in students' perceived strengths and weakness in mathematics.
   - whether they have expanded their view about the content of mathematics.
   - growth in their attitude towards mathematics.
   - whether they have learned new approaches to problem-solving.
   - how they use mathematics in their daily lives.
   - whether they have grown in their ability to express themselves in print.
   - the effectiveness of your mathematics program.
5. Compare each student's response to *Questions for Reflection* at the beginning of the school year.

From the Classroom

In September, the student writes how she learned about multiplication and division.

In June, her view of mathematics has expanded to include the application of mathematical concepts in real-life situations. She emphasized the need to be persistent and choose an appropriate strategy to solve a problem. Her focus on the process rather than the solution helped build confidence in her ability to solve problems and apply mathematical ideas. She recognizes the need to communicate her ideas effectively in print.

I learned about multiplication and division.

I want to learn about fractions.

September

I learned that you need to be persistent in problem solving. Let's say there's a problem that says: 20 birds lived in a zoo. they had only 9 cages. how many in each? If you worked on it for 10 minutes. keep working. That's what persistent means. I also learned that you should find a way that is easy for you to solve problems. For the problem above. let's say drawing pictures is they way you tried.

I'm pretty well rounded in math but I'd like to work on doing harder problems with higher numbers. I also need to work on writing more about the subject I'm working on to tell what I'm thinking.

June

Suggestions For Other Assessment Questions

Perimeter

- Write a definition for perimeter.
- Draw a rectangle with a perimeter of 12 inches and label the length of each side. Explain how you found the length of each side. Is there another way to draw a rectangle with a perimeter of 12 inches?
- Why do you think it is important to learn about perimeter?
- What other mathematics did you use?

Graph Interpretation

- What is the purpose of the graph?
- What does the graph tell you?
- What comparisons can you make?
- How did you organize the data?

Pentominoes

- What is a pentomino?
- What did you learn about pentominoes?
- How are the pentominoes alike?
- How are the pentominoes different?

Patterns

- What is a pattern?
- What are some patterns you see on a hundred chart?
- How can patterns help you solve a mathematical problem?

How Many Ways? *(Discrete Mathematics)*

- If you have three flavors of ice cream, how many different double scoop ice cream cones could you make?
  How did you solve the problem?
  Is there another way you could have solved the problem?
  What patterns did you see?
  What if there were four flavors of ice cream?

Fifth Grade

Questions For Reflection
What I Already Know About Mathematics

Math Exploration 1
Fractions
Literature Connection: *Eight Hands Round*

Math Exploration 2
Baker's Dozen (Writing Word Problems)
Literature Connection: *The Baker's Dozen*

Questions for Reflection
What I Learned About Mathematics

Suggestions For Other Assessment Questions

Questions for Reflection

1. At the beginning of the school year, pose the following questions:

Questions For Reflection
What I Already Know About Mathematics • What is mathematics? • What did you learn in mathematics last year? (Give examples) • Did you like math last year? Why? • How do you use mathematics in your daily life? • What helps you learn best? • What do you hope to learn in mathematics this year?

2. Have students discuss the questions as a total group. Record their ideas on the board.
3. Have students answer the questions in their journals.
   ★ *Encourage students to use diagrams, graphs, pictures and symbols to help explain their answers.*
4. The journal entries will give you information about:
   - students' perceived strengths and weakness in mathematics.
   - how they define the content of mathematics.
   - their attitude towards mathematics.
   - their approach to problem-solving.
   - how they use mathematics in their daily lives.
5. Save the journal entries and use them to compare each student's response to *Questions for Reflection* at the end of the school year. (See *From the Classroom,* page 109).

Math Exploration 1: Fractions

Literature Connection: *Eight Hands Round* by Ann Whitford Paul
The letters of the alphabet are introduced with names of early American patchwork quilt patterns. The origin of each design is described.

1. Tell students they will be studying about fractions. Ask these questions:
   - What are fractions?
   - How do we use fractions in our daily lives?
2. Read orally *Eight Hands Round.* Discuss the quilt patterns using fractional language. *Example:* The quilt pattern is divided into 4 equal parts. About half the quilt pattern is red.
3. Students can make their own quilt patterns by folding a 4″ by 4″ white construction paper into equal parts in a variety of ways. They can color the equal parts and describe the designs using fractional language. The quilt patterns can be mounted to form a class quilt.

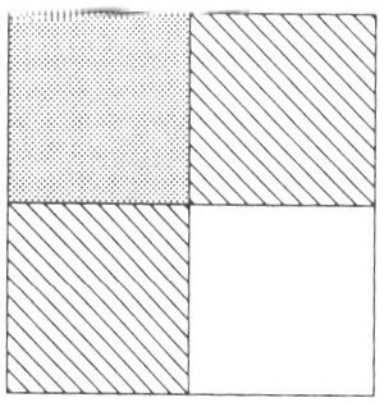

4. During the unit on fractions, provide these hands-on opportunities:
   - Talk about fractional parts using concrete materials. This will provide opportunities for students to use fractional language. (What fraction of our class are girls? What fraction of your last name are vowels? What fraction of these jelly beans are red?)
   - Students can make fraction strips for one whole, $\frac{1}{2}$, $\frac{1}{4}$ and $\frac{1}{8}$. They need to use a different color construction paper strip (3″ by 18″) for each fraction. Students fold, cut and label the fractions. Then they make observations using their strips to compare fractions, find equivalent fractions and write fraction sentences.

<table>
<tr><td colspan="8">one whole</td></tr>
<tr><td colspan="4">$\frac{1}{2}$</td><td colspan="4">$\frac{1}{2}$</td></tr>
<tr><td colspan="2">$\frac{1}{4}$</td><td colspan="2">$\frac{1}{4}$</td><td colspan="2">$\frac{1}{4}$</td><td colspan="2">$\frac{1}{4}$</td></tr>
<tr><td>$\frac{1}{8}$</td><td>$\frac{1}{8}$</td><td>$\frac{1}{8}$</td><td>$\frac{1}{8}$</td><td>$\frac{1}{8}$</td><td>$\frac{1}{8}$</td><td>$\frac{1}{8}$</td><td>$\frac{1}{8}$</td></tr>
</table>

From the Classroom: *Sample 5*

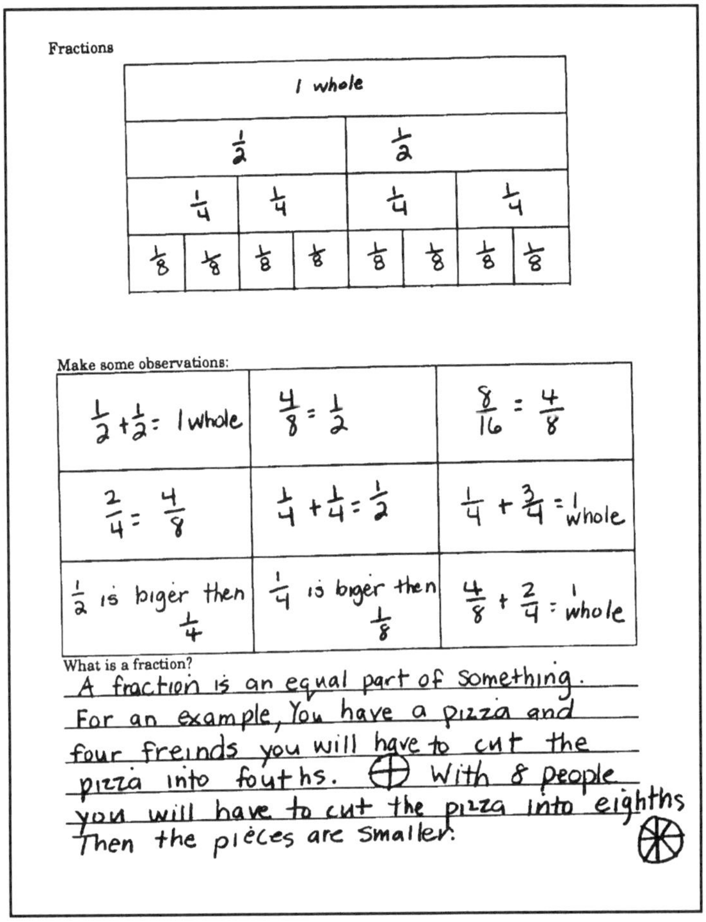

Fractions

1 whole							
$\frac{1}{2}$				$\frac{1}{2}$			
$\frac{1}{4}$		$\frac{1}{4}$		$\frac{1}{4}$		$\frac{1}{4}$	
$\frac{1}{8}$	$\frac{1}{8}$	$\frac{1}{8}$	$\frac{1}{8}$	$\frac{1}{8}$	$\frac{1}{8}$	$\frac{1}{8}$	$\frac{1}{8}$

Make some observations:

$\frac{1}{2}+\frac{1}{2}=$ 1 whole	$\frac{4}{8}=\frac{1}{2}$	$\frac{8}{16}=\frac{4}{8}$
$\frac{2}{4}=\frac{4}{8}$	$\frac{1}{4}+\frac{1}{4}=\frac{1}{2}$	$\frac{1}{4}+\frac{3}{4}=1$ whole
$\frac{1}{2}$ is biger then $\frac{1}{4}$	$\frac{1}{4}$ is biger then $\frac{1}{8}$	$\frac{4}{8}+\frac{2}{4}=1$ whole

What is a fraction?

A fraction is an equal part of something. For an example, You have a pizza and four freinds you will have to cut the pizza into fouths. With 8 people you will have to cut the pizza into eighths Then the pieces are smaller.

Here, the student demonstrates her ability to compare fractions, find equivalent fractions and write fraction sentences as she explores the concept using manipulatives. The task requires the student to define a fraction based on her observations.

- Use pattern blocks to name fractions, compare fractions, find equivalent fractions and write fraction sentences.

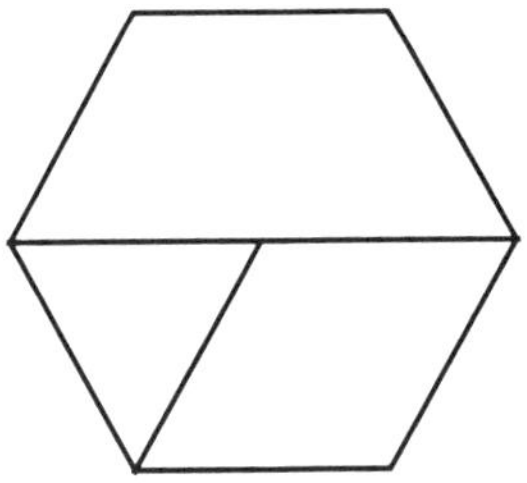

- Use geoboards and rubber bands to show fractions by dividing the geoboard in a variety of ways. Students can record their solutions on Activity Sheet 5-A. *Example:* How many different ways could you divide the geoboard in half?

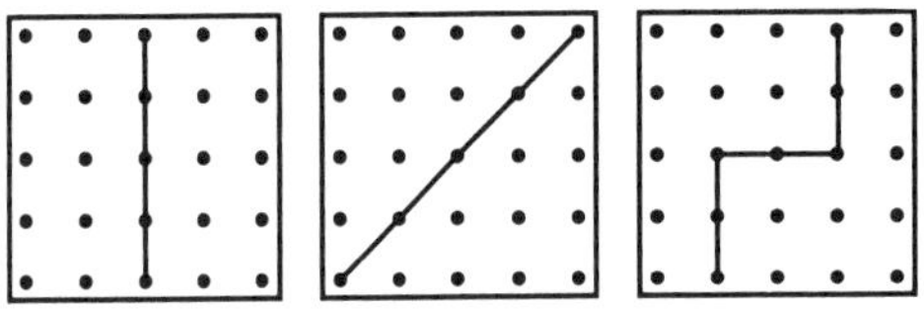

Then have students prove in writing, how they know that the board is exactly divided in half.

Students can work in groups to solve word problems involving fractional parts and explain their strategies. Examples:

- Janet planted some flowers in her garden. She had 2 dozen roses. $\frac{1}{2}$ are pink. How many roses are pink?
- Jim ate $\frac{2}{3}$ of the 12 doughnuts. How many doughnuts did he eat?
- Jerome bought some cookies. $\frac{1}{3}$ were oatmeal, $\frac{1}{2}$ were chocolate and the rest were sugar. There were 5 oatmeal cookies. How many cookies were there?

5. When the unit on fractions is complete, pose the following discussion questions about fractions:

Discussion Questions: Fractions

- What are fractions?
- How do we use fractions in our daily lives?
- Draw a picture to show that $\frac{5}{9}$ of the shapes are circles.
- Explain why $\frac{1}{2}$ equals $\frac{4}{8}$.
- Which is more $\frac{3}{5}$ or $\frac{4}{9}$? Explain how you got your answer.
- Solve the problem $\frac{3}{4} + \frac{2}{6}$. Show what the problem means with writing and pictures.
- Do you think you are good at solving problems using fractions? Why?

6. Have students answer the questions in their journals.
   ★ *Encourage students to use diagrams, charts and pictures to help explain their answers.*
7. Use journal entries to assess students' level of understanding of fractions and their ability to express what they know. The following examples demonstrate a range of student responses that is likely to occur in your classroom.

From the Classroom: *Sample 5–2*

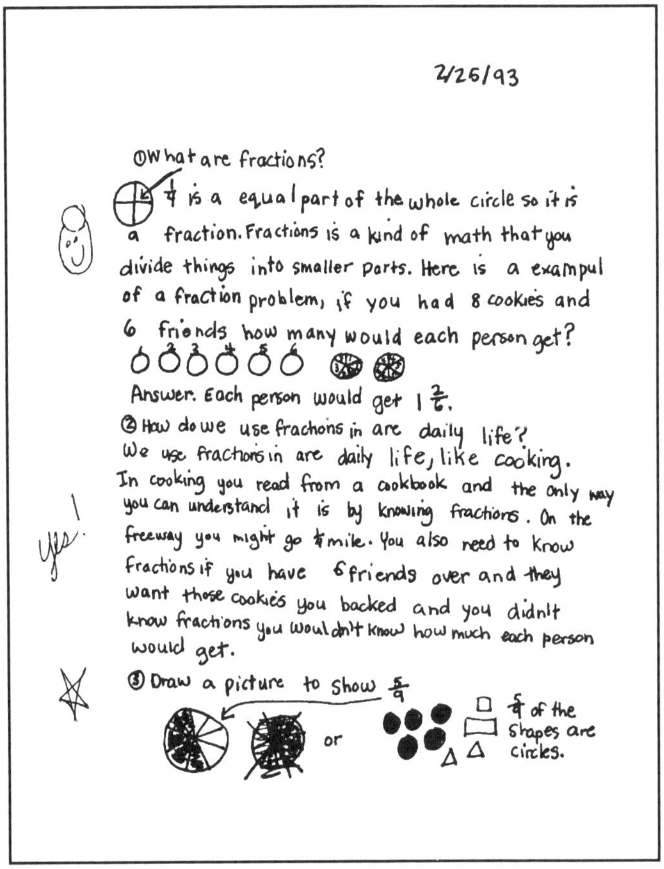

2/26/93

① What are fractions?

$\frac{1}{4}$ is a equal part of the whole circle so it is a fraction. Fractions is a kind of math that you divide things into smaller parts. Here is a exampul of a fraction problem, if you had 8 cookies and 6 friends how many would each person get?

Answer. Each person would get $1\frac{2}{6}$.

② How do we use frachons in are daily life?

We use fractions in are daily life, like cooking. In cooking you read from a cookbook and the only way you can understand it is by knowing fractions. On the freeway you might go $\frac{1}{4}$ mile. You also need to know fractions if you have 6 friends over and they want those cookies you backed and you didn't know fractions you wouldn't know how much each person would get.

Yes!

③ Draw a picture to show $\frac{5}{9}$

or

$\frac{5}{9}$ of the shapes are circles.

page 1

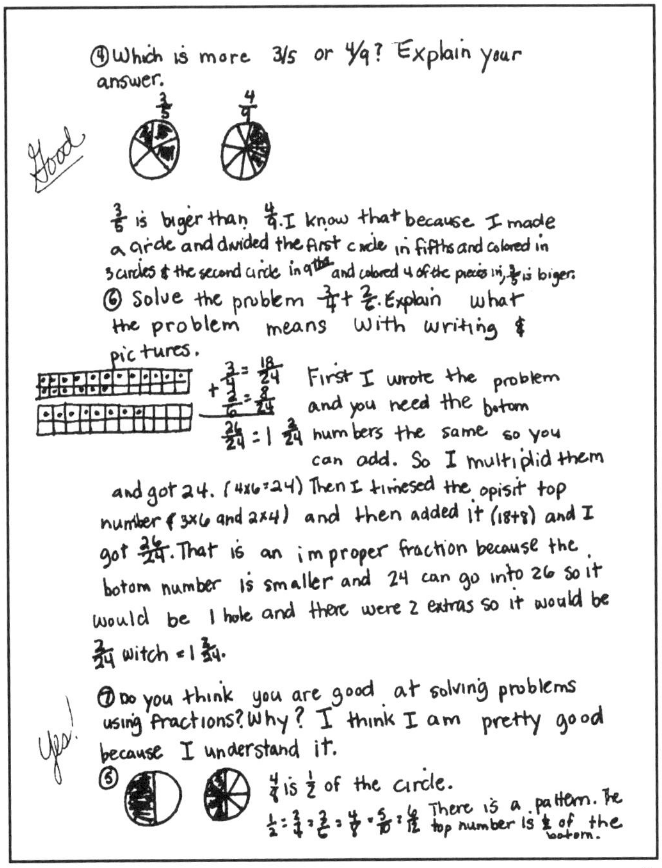

④ Which is more 3/5 or 4/9? Explain your answer.

Good

$\frac{3}{5}$ is biger than $\frac{4}{9}$. I know that because I made a circle and divided the first circle in fifths and colored in 3 circles & the second circle in 9ths and colored 4 of the pieces in, $\frac{3}{5}$ is biger.

⑥ Solve the problem $\frac{3}{4}+\frac{2}{6}$. Explain what the problem means with writing & pictures.

$\frac{3}{4}=\frac{18}{24}$, $+\frac{2}{6}=\frac{8}{24}$, $\frac{26}{24}=1\frac{2}{24}$

First I wrote the problem and you need the botom numbers the same so you can add. So I multiplid them and got 24. (4x6=24) Then I timesed the opisit top number (3x6 and 2x4) and then added it (18+8) and I got $\frac{26}{24}$. That is an improper fraction because the botom number is smaller and 24 can go into 26 so it would be 1 hole and there were 2 extras so it would be $\frac{26}{24}$ witch = $1\frac{2}{24}$.

⑦ Do you think you are good at solving problems using fractions? Why? I think I am pretty good because I understand it.

Yes!

⑤ $\frac{4}{8}$ is $\frac{1}{2}$ of the circle.

$\frac{1}{2}=\frac{2}{4}=\frac{3}{6}=\frac{4}{8}=\frac{5}{10}=\frac{6}{12}$ There is a pattern. The top number is $\frac{1}{2}$ of the botom.

page 2

In this sample, the student answered all discussion questions completely. Pictures were used to help explain answers. She seems to have a firm understanding of the concept of fractions. However, she needs more experience with equivalent fractions and lowest common denominator to help when performing operations with fractions.

From the Classroom: *Sample 5–3*

In this sample, the student demonstrates some knowledge of fractions but all questions are not answered completely and ideas need further explanation. There are no apparent misunderstandings. However, the student needs to add more detail to demonstrate full competence in expressing his ideas. He does not explain why $3/5$ is bigger than $4/9$ and his definition of fractions does not include the idea of ***equal*** *parts of a whole.*

2/25/93

① What are fractions?
Good
Fractions are parts of one whole thing.

② How do we use fractions in our daily lives? if you go to a store it is much easyer to buy something you can divide up.

③ Draw a picture to show 5/9.

④ Explain why 1/2 equals 4/8? because if you put 1/2 into 4/8 it would work.

⑤ Which is more 3/5 or 4/9? Explain your answer. The answer is 3/5.

Draw a picture to see if you're right.

⑥ Solve the problem $\frac{3}{4} + \frac{2}{6}$ show what the problem means.

$\frac{3}{4} = \frac{18}{24}$

$+ \frac{2}{6} = \frac{8}{24}$

$\frac{26}{24} = 1\frac{2}{24} = 1\frac{1}{12}$

You have to multiple and add.

page 1

⑦ Do you think you are good at solving problems using fractions? Why? I think that I am ok at solving problems because it takes me a while to figer the problem out but once I get it I do ok.

You do very well once you get it!

page 2

How many different ways can you divide a geoboard in ____________________?

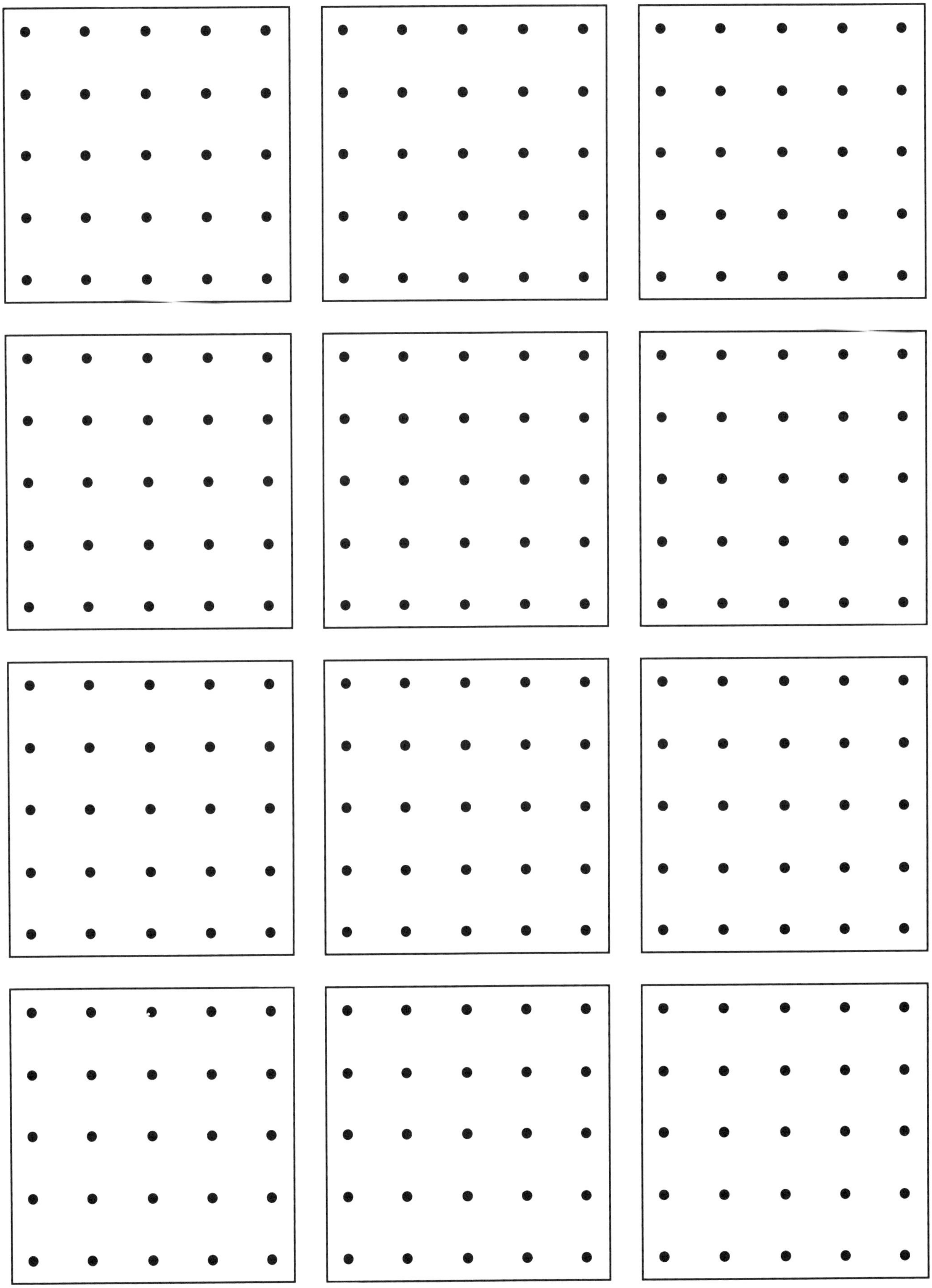

Math Exploration 2: Bakers Dozen *(Writing Word Problems)*

Literature Connection: *The Baker's Dozen* by Heather Forest
A greedy baker learns about the joy of giving from a mysterious old woman who insists that a dozen means thirteen cookies.

1. Read orally *The Baker's Dozen*. Discuss the problem in the story and how it was solved. Talk about how our lives would be different if a dozen was 13 instead of 12. Ask these questions:
   - How many cookies would be in a ½ baker's dozen? ¼ baker's dozen?
   - How many more cookies would you get if you bought 26 baker's dozens?
   - What problems might occur if we used a "baker's dozen?"
2. **Introduce the Problem**
   If Yummy Bakery sold a dozen cookies for every baker's dozen Star Bakery sold, how many cookies would Star Bakery sell when Yummy bakery sold 168?
   How many dozen cookies did each bakery sell?
3. Students need to discuss the problem and work in pairs to solve the problem. (Students can record their ideas in their math journals.)
4. Have students share how they solved the problem. Discuss different strategies and the mathematics used.

   Example:

Yummy Bakery	12	24	36	48	60	72	84	96	108	120	132	144	156	168
Star Bakery	13	26	39	52	65	78	91	104	117	130	143	156	169	182

From the Classroom: *Sample 5–1*

Here, the student is able to solve the problem and explain his solution with symbols and words. The task requires the student to choose a strategy and justify his mathematical thinking. It helps the student to see that there is more than one way to solve a problem.

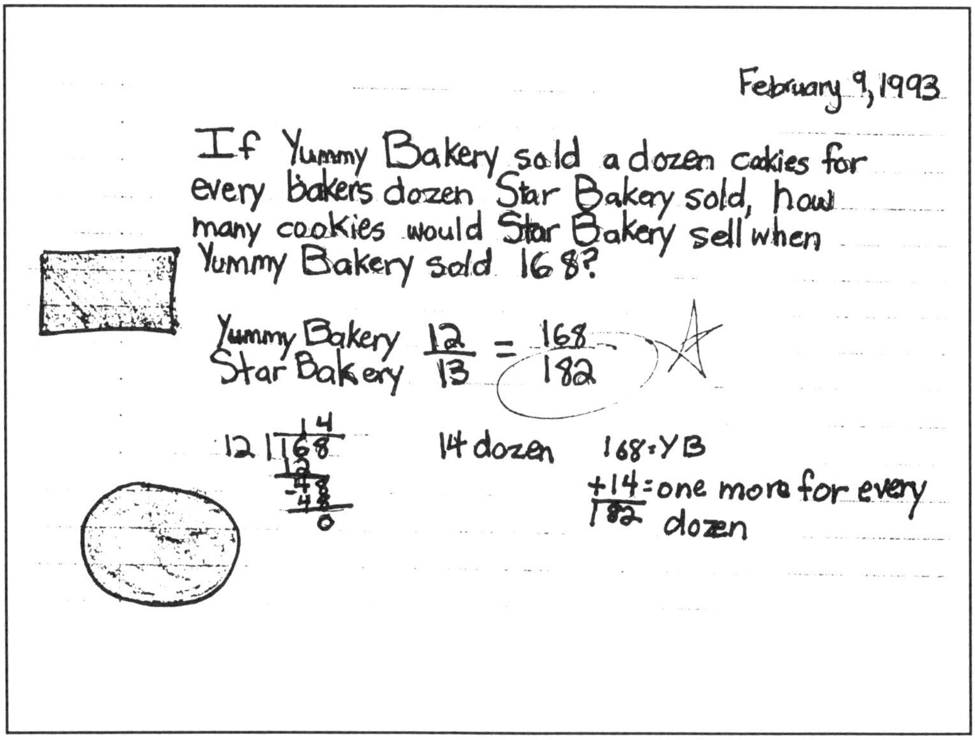
February 9, 1993

If Yummy Bakery sold a dozen cokies for every bakers dozen Star Bakery sold, how many cookies would Star Bakery sell when Yummy Bakery sold 168?

Yummy Bakery / Star Bakery $\frac{12}{13} = \frac{168}{182}$

12 ⟌168 = 14

14 dozen

168 = YB
+14 = one more for every dozen
182

5. Have students brainstorm ideas for other story problems they could write using a "baker's dozen."
6. **Instructions for Students**
   Work in pairs to write two of your own story problems using a baker's dozen. Write the problem and show your work. Explain strategies used to solve the problem.

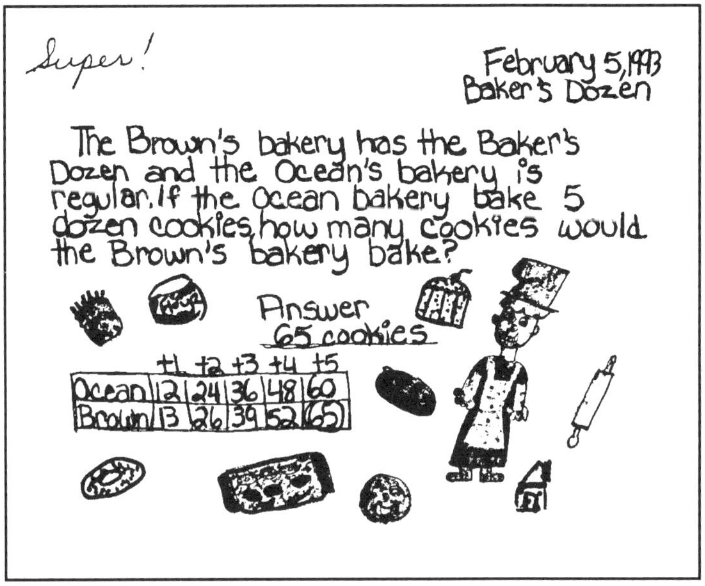

Super!

February 5, 1993
Baker's Dozen

The Brown's bakery has the Baker's Dozen and the Ocean's bakery is regular. If the Ocean bakery bake 5 dozen cookies, how many cookies would the Brown's bakery bake?

Answer
65 cookies

	+1	+2	+3	+4	+5
Ocean	12	24	36	48	60
Brown	13	26	39	52	(65)

From the Classroom: *Sample 5–4*

In Samples 5–4 and 5–5, the students demonstrate their ability to create a word problem that utilizes mathematical concepts. The task requires the students to synthesize what they know about mathematical concepts and explain their thinking. The first sample was similar to the problem given in class. The second sample provides a more thorough explanation of the child's thinking.

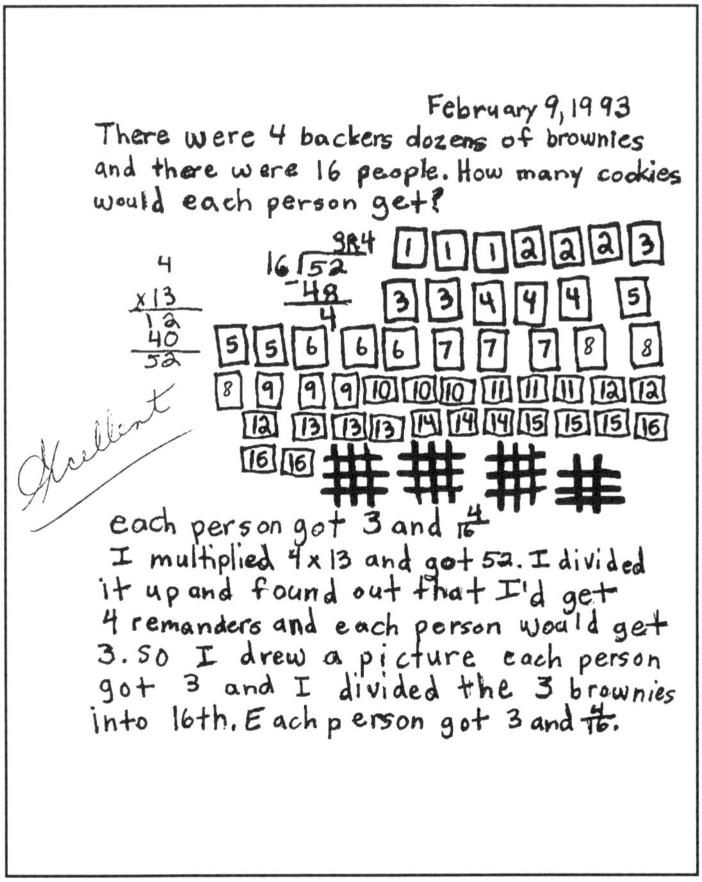

February 9, 1993

There were 4 backers dozens of brownies and there were 16 people. How many cookies would each person get?

4 × 13 = 52

16 ÷ 52 = 3 R 4

Excellent

each person got 3 and $\frac{4}{16}$

I multiplied 4 x 13 and got 52. I divided it up and found out that I'd get 4 remanders and each person would get 3. So I drew a picture each person got 3 and I divided the 3 brownies into 16th. Each person got 3 and $\frac{4}{16}$.

From the Classroom: *Sample 5–5*

7. Students can trade problems with other groups and see how they would solve their problems.
8. Discuss the following questions with the class:

Discussion Questions: Baker's Dozen

- What was the problem in the story?
- How could a *baker's dozen* change our lives mathematically?
- If you bought 27½ *baker's dozen* cookies for a school party, how many extra cookies would you get? Explain how you got your answer.
- Write one of your own *baker's dozen* problems. Show how you solved the problem. Explain the strategies you used and the mathematics.
- How does writing your own story problem help you to be a better problem solver?

9. Have students answer the questions in their journals.
   ★ *Encourage students to use diagrams, charts, pictures and symbols to help explain their answers.*
10. Use journal entries to assess students' ability to select an appropriate problem solving strategy and describe it coherently. Students must be able to apply mathematical concepts to solve the problem. The emphasis here is more on the child's ability to communicate the process than on the correct answer.

From the Classroom: *Sample 5–6*

page 1

*In this sample, the student answers all questions completely. His **baker's dozen** problem and solution demonstrate an in-depth understanding of mathematical concepts. Mathematical ideas are communicated clearly and effectively.*

Sample 5–6: *continued*

Feb 10, 1993

1. The problem in the story "Baker's Dozen" was that the baker did not put 13 cookies in the bag for the old lady. He put 12 when she asked for 13. When he started putting in an extra measure his bussiness skyrocketed.

2. If baker's dozens were used regularly in the world it would change the way we eat. For if you wanted to have half a bakers dozen you would get half a cookie (plus 6 more cookies). Wouldn't that be strange?

Great!

3.

```
   27.5              27.5             357.5 (bakers dozen)
 ×   12 cookies    ×   13 cookies   − 330.0 (dozen)
    550               825               27.5
   2750              2750
   330.0 cookies     357.5 cookies     27.5 (27 1/2) more cookies
```

page 2

It's the same awnser that I started with, because you get one more cookie with every bakers dozen, for example if you had 35 ½ bakers dozens you would get 35 ½ extra cookies. Wouldn't that be a deal!

4. Writting my own story problem helped me be a better problem solver because it helped me find easeir ways to solve a problem and that my brain works faster than my hand. I have to think before I write!

Good advice!

page 3

From the Classroom: *Sample 5–7*

In this sample, the student communicates her ideas successfully. Her ***baker's dozen*** *problem and solution demonstrate a good understanding of mathematical concepts. However, the mathematics are not as sophisticated as sample 5–6.*

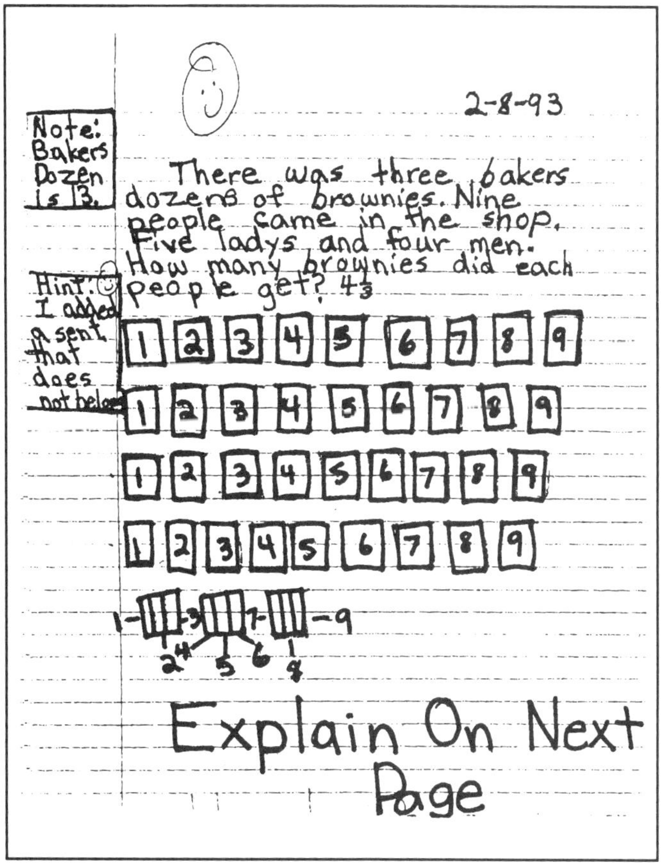
2-8-93

Note: Bakers Dozen is 13.

There was three bakers dozens of brownies. Nine people came in the shop. Five ladys and four men. How many brownies did each people get? $4\frac{1}{3}$

Hint: I added a sent that does not belong

Explain On Next Page

page 1

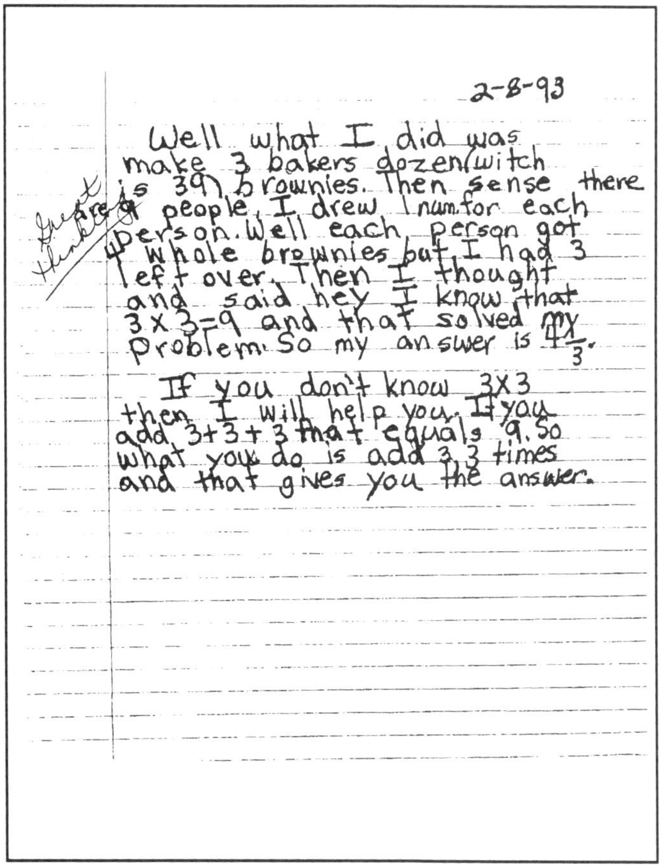
2-8-93

Well what I did was make 3 bakers dozen (witch is 39) brownies. Then sense there are 9 people, I drew 1 num for each person. Well each person got 4 whole brownies but I had 3 left over. Then I thought and said hey I know that 3x3=9 and that solved my problem. So my answer is $4\frac{1}{3}$.

If you don't know 3X3 then I will help you. If you add 3+3+3 that equals 9. So what you do is add 3 3 times and that gives you the answer.

Great thinking

page 2

Sample 5–7: *continued*

2-10-93

1. What was the problem in the story?

I think the problem was that the Baker said a dozen is 12 and the lady said a dozen is 13 but the Baker didn't belive that and only gave her 12. So the lady put a curse on the Baker.

2. How would a Backer's Dozen comeflicked in math?

Well if you asked for a half of dozen of cookies you would get 6 and a half. Somebody may not want a half of cookie. Another reson is you couldnt split a dozen cookies between 2, 3, 4, 5, 6, 7, 8, 9, 10, 11 or 12 people without spliting them in half. Even if you try to split it in half it wouldn't be even because the cookie always crumbles, Then its not even. *It would be a problem*

page 3

2-11-93

3. If you bought 27 ½ bakers dozen cookies for a school party how many extra cookies would you get? 27 ½

1.
```
   2
  27
 x13
  81
 270
 351
```

2.
```
  351
 +  6 1/2
  357 1/2
```

3. [scribbled out]

```
   27
  x12
   54
  270
  324
 +  6
  330
```

```
 357 1/2
 330
 027 1/2
```

Yes! Well how I got it was thought well 27 ½ - 1 each bakers dozen then you get your answer so the answer is 27 ½.

4. How does writing your own story problem help you to be a better problem solver?

Well it helps you learn tricks about fractions. It also makes you think about how your going to solve your problem. ☆

page 4

Questions for Reflection

1. At the end of the school year, pose the following questions:

Discussion Questions: How Many Rabbits?

What I Learned About Mathematics

- What is mathematics?
- Did you like math this year? Why?
- What did you learn about mathematics this year? (give examples)
- What do you still need to work on in mathematics?
- What math activities did you like best?
- How do you use mathematics in your daily life?
- What would you like to learn in mathematics next year?

2. Have students discuss the questions as a total group. Record their ideas on the board.
3. Have students write in their journals.
   ★ *Encourage students to use diagrams, graphs, pictures and symbols to help explain their answers.*
4. Compare students' responses to their journal entry on *What I Already Know About Mathematics.* You will gain information about:
   - changes in student's perceived strengths and weakness in mathematics.
   - whether they have expanded their view about the content of mathematics.
   - growth in their attitude towards mathematics.
   - whether they have learned new approaches to problem-solving.
   - how they use mathematics in their daily lives.
   - whether they have grown in their ability to express themselves in print.
   - the effectiveness of your mathematics program.
5. Compare each student's response to *Questions for Reflection* at the beginning of the school year.

From the Classroom: *Grade 5*

In September, the student sees mathematics as the study of numbers.

In June, his view of mathematics is expanded to move beyond numbers to include geometry, measurement, collecting data and solving problems in our daily lives. He expresses the need to communicate effectively in print so he can explain his mathematical thinking and emphasize his process.

Mathematics is a combination of many things like how to use numbers.
You use math to count money. on homework and in tests.

September

Mathematics is all around us. You will need mathematics the rest of your life to solve problems like how much the Cowboys are beating the Lions by in football or if your new desk will fit in your room. It is numbers and shapes and charts and graphs. You will explain how you got your answer when you write in math.
Every sport is made out of math because of the shape of the field. When you are cutting up food you use math to enough enough food for each person.When you are getting ready for school, you see how much time you have left.

June

Suggestions For Other Assessment Questions

How Many Different Rectangular Arrays Can You Make Using 72 Tiles?

- How did you solve the problem?
- Is there another way you could have solved the problem?
- Describe the rectangular arrays.
- How do you know you found all the possible solutions?
- What mathematics did you learn?
- How did you feel about the problem?
- How did you work cooperatively with other group members?

Area and Perimeter Investigation: Do Rectangles With Equal Perimeter Have Equal Areas?

Use tiles to make as many different rectangles as you can with a perimeter of 24 and draw a picture of each rectangle.

- Describe each rectangle. (Make a chart to describe each rectangle.)

Example:

Length	Width	Area
11	1	11
10	2	20

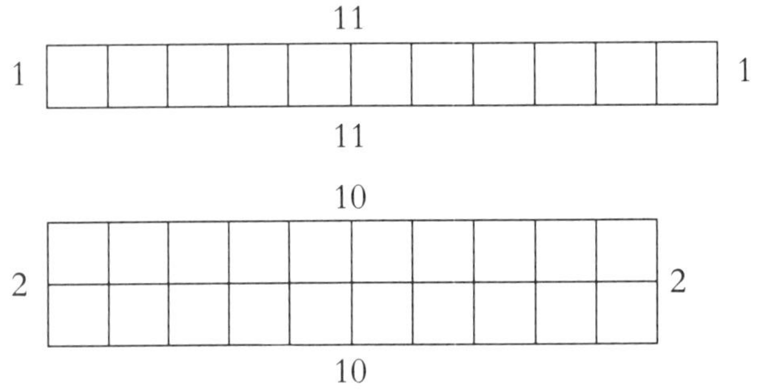

What patterns do you see on the chart?

- What was the area of each rectangle?
- How did you find the area of each rectangle?
- Do rectangles with equal perimeters have equal areas? Explain.

Multiples

- What is a multiple?
- Name some multiples of 4.
- How do you know they are multiples of 4?
- How can knowing multiples help you in mathematics?

How Many Ways? *(Discrete Mathematics)*

How many ways can Bill, Carla, Jenna and Tom sit on a bench in a different order?

- How did you solve the problem?
- Is there another way you could have solved the problem?
- What patterns did you see?
- How did you feel about the problem?
- What if there were 5 children sitting on the bench?

What I Already Know About Decimals

- What is a decimal?
- How do we use decimals in real-life?
- How can fractions help you understand decimals?
- Draw a picture to represent .4 and .04. Which is more?

Bibliography Of Children's Literature

Bogart, Jo Ellen, *10 For Dinner,* Scholastic Inc., NY, 1989.

Briggs, Raymond, *Jim & the Beanstalk,* Sandcastle Books, Putnam Publishing Group, NY, 1970.

Cleveland, David, *The April Rabbits,* Scholastic Inc., NY, 1986.

Crews, Donald, *Ten Black Dots,* Greenwillow Books, William Morrow Co., NY, 1986.

Dee, Ruby, *Two Ways To Count To Ten,* H. Holt & Co., NY, 1988.

Demi, *Demi's Count the Animals 1-2-3,* Grosset & Dunlap, Putnam Publishing Group, NY, 1986.

Forest, Heather, *The Baker's Dozen,* Harcourt Brace Jovanovich, San Diego, CA, 1993.

Hamm, Diane Johnston, *How Many Feet In The Bed?,* Simon & Schuster, NY, 1991.

Hulme, Joy N., *Sea Squares,* Hyperion Books, Walt Disney Book Publishing Group, NY, 1991.

Lottridge, Celia Barker, *One Watermelon Seed,* Oxford University Press, NY, 1990.

Maestro, Betsy and Giulio Maestro, *Dollars and Cents for Harriet,* Crown Publishers, Inc., NY, 1988.

Moore, Inga, *Six Dinner Sid,* Simon & Schuster, NY, 1991.

Paul, Ann Whitford, *Eight Hands Round: A Patchwork Alphabet,* Harper Collins, NY, 1991.

Pryor, Ainslie, *The Baby Blue Cat and The Whole Batch of Cookies,* Viking Penguin, NY, 1991.

Samton, Sheila White, *Moon To Sun: An Adding Book,* Caroline House/Boyds Mills Press, Inc., Honesdale, PA, 1991.

Testa, Fulvio, *If You Look Around You,* Dial Books for Young Readers, Penguin U.S.A., NY, 1987.

Van Fleet, Matthew, *One Yellow Lion: Foldout Fun with Numbers, Colors, Animals,* Dial Books for Young Readers, Penguin U.S.A., NY, 1992.

Wylie, Joanne & David, *A Fishy Shape Story,* Children's Press, Grollier, Inc., Chicago, IL, 1986.